Say Goodbye to Your PDI

Say Goodbye to your

PDI

(Personality Disordered Individual)

Recognize People Who Make
You Miserable and Eliminate Them
from Your Life for Good!

Stan Kapuchinski, M.D.

Health Communications, Inc.
Deerfield Beach, Florida

www.hcibooks.com

BP53

Library of Congress Cataloging-in-Publication Data

Kapuchinski, Stan.

Say goodbye to your PDI (Personality Disordered Individuals) : recognize people who make you miserable and eliminate them from your life—for good / Stan Kapuchinski.

    p. cm.

    Includes bibliographical references and index.

    ISBN-13: 978-0-7573-0615-0 (trade paper)

    ISBN-10: 0-7573-0615-2 (trade paper)

    1. Personality disorders—Patients.   2. Psychotherapy.   I. Title.

RC554.K37 2007

616.89'14—dc22

                                         2007016690

Publisher: Health Communications, Inc.
             3201 S.W. 15th Street
             Deerfield Beach, FL 33442–8190

Book Cover Design by Larissa Hise Henoch
Interior book design and formatting by Dawn Von Strolley Grove

3/1/11

To My Extraordinary Family
Each So Unique and Wonderful
Sue
Matt
Sara
Who Give Me Their Love

Contents

Acknowledgments

Every physician knows—or should know—that it is from his patients that he learns about his art. The patients I have had the privilege to treat have taught me and continue to teach me about the human soul. I am indebted to them for their sharing of their experiences, some of which I have adapted for this book. I continue to be in awe of an individual's resiliency to carry on, to change, and to seek happiness.

I am especially grateful for the PDIs who continue to thrive in our world. I am not thankful if I have to deal with one of these manipulative people, but I must remember that it is their unending quality of making other people miserable that allowed me to write this book.

Many thanks go to my agent, Sharlene Martin of Martin Literary Agency, whose drive, great business acumen, and wisdom have been a guiding force for me and who continues to remind me to check my spelling. Throughout the process of getting this book out, Michele Mastrisciani of Health Communications has been enthusiastic, quick, insightful, encouraging, and so very easy to deal with . . . along with having a great sense of humor.

Additionally, I want to express my deep respect and admiration for the people at Health Communications, who have been so helpful, encouraging, and genuinely caring in publishing this book.

I am also indebted to various colleagues, family members, and friends who suffered through reading parts of this book and helped with their opinions and advice.

Introduction

Misery conjures up in our minds thoughts of unhappiness, wretchedness, and gloom. Millions of us are miserable and frustrated on a daily basis because of having to deal with difficult and trying individuals in our professional, business, or personal lives. This book will definitely help you deal more effectively with the users, the manipulators, the smooth talkers, and the guilt-trippers out there with whom we must interact and who can make us feel miserable in the process. These people often have unique attitude problems and behaviors that can collectively be called personality disorders.

Personality disordered individuals (PDIs) are extremely manipulative. They trap us in prolonged relationships and keep us there despite how unhappy we feel in them. No matter how hard we try to improve the situation, things do not change. Unfairly blaming ourselves for the dismal state of things, we find ourselves stuck. We are forever miserable as we try to endure, not knowing where we failed. What's worse is that we are continually angry over our powerlessness to change our situation.

This book addresses many miserable situations that might occur every day in your professional, business, or work life, as well as in your personal life. It also guides you in what you can and cannot do in dealing with these irritating, demanding, and wearisome people. With a better sense of control in your life, you will be happier each day.

Chapter 1 explains PDIs in general and how they ensnare you into repeatedly dealing with them. The remaining chapters illustrate the various and unique types of PDIs to help you recognize them. Each chapter describes the specific behavioral style of a particular controlling type of personality disorder and provides *True-Life Adventure* examples from professional, business, and personal settings to help you fully picture in your mind the unique type of problem behaviors you may be encountering.

Each chapter also shows how you can further recognize the effect that each individual personality disorder has on you by listing the various feelings that may rise up within you when dealing with one of these manipulative individuals. Identifying these feelings is extremely important because these psychological villains trap you by manipulating your feelings and reactions. This book explains how PDIs use these feelings against you to keep you in a relationship with them. Once you identify how you are being ensnared, you are better armed to elude the web that the PDI is spinning for you.

Chapters 2–6 help you to key in on:

• The PDIs' basic behaviors and manipulations
• How PDIs make you feel
• What to do and, often more important, what not to do in how you behave

Throughout the book, I have listed *Remember* points to stress key things for you to hold in your mind when you deal with a PDI.

As you become more knowledgeable and confident in handling these difficult people, you will feel a better sense of control. Feeling more in charge will allow you to feel less miserable. You will then feel happier about yourself and how you are handling your life.

The examples in this book are based to a large degree on people whom I have encountered in my practice of psychiatry and in my personal and business lives. Sometimes I have intentionally created a composite portrait to illustrate a particular point. I have tried to keep the definitions and terms as practical and down to earth as possible. The diagnoses, definitions, and descriptions of the personality disorders are based on psychiatric terms as defined in *The Diagnostic and Statistical Manual IV* published by the American Psychiatric Association.

THE BASICS: ELIMINATING MISERY

A good day is one in which we do not meet too many unpleasant, angry, contrary, weird, unhappy, nasty, guiltifying, or callous people. If we come across them, hopefully the encounter is brief and isolated. This book, however, deals with those objectionable people in our daily lives with whom we must deal and who do not enrich, improve, enhance, boost, encourage, motivate, or inspire us but who—*day in and day out*—make us *miserable . . .*

people with more deep-seated problems in getting along with others: personality disordered individuals (PDIs).

This book is written for all of you who have to endure the demands, the control, the mind games, the manipulations, and the frustrations that encompass everyday life when dealing with a PDI in your professional, business, and personal lives. In psychiatry, an old adage about personality disorders says, "Neurotic people make *themselves* miserable. People with personality disorders make *everyone* else miserable!" If you remember anything else from this book, remember that!

People with personality disorders definitely stir up a not-so-pleasant feeling in us. What can be confusing is that sometimes after we first meet them, we might feel quite grand, awed, elevated, charmed, or pleased to be in their company, depending on the particular type of PDI you meet. However, whether the miserable feeling you get comes sooner or later, when dealing with a PDI, the misery *always* happens.

WHY THIS BOOK WAS WRITTEN

As we encounter the PDIs who make us miserable in our everyday lives, we feel discouraged in not being able to make things better or to work things out to improve the relationship. We feel trapped, angry, powerless, and manipulated. We also feel guilty and frustrated in not being able to solve this problem that seems beyond our control. Sometimes, the PDI so manipulates us that we are confused, unhappy, and discontented . . . and we do not know why. In short, every day we dread being with these people, but feel helpless in finding a way out.

Never fear, help is at hand.
You can break out of this cycle of misery.

This book is written to help you recognize the PDI and how he or she cleverly manipulates and exploits you. With that knowledge, you will become much smarter in dealing with the PDI and feel more in control of your life.

WHAT THIS BOOK WILL SHOW YOU

Chapter 1 of this book takes a general approach to a number of different topics:

1. What you should know about personality disordered individuals and how they cause misery in others. Specifically, you'll learn:

   - What a personality disorder is.
   - How a personality disorder individual (PDI) behaves.
   - How PDIs affect you.
   - How you get trapped and manipulated by the PDI's behavior.
   - Why you stay trapped.

2. How to recognize a person with a personality disorder (so you will not get trapped):

   - Analyze your feelings.

3. The prime things to remember in dealing with a PDI:

   - The basics about PDIs.
   - What you can and cannot do—the most important element to remember in dealing with PDIs.

4. Descriptions of those who are most trapped by PDIs:

   - The caring person.
   - The rescuer.
   - The guilty person.
   - The giving person.
   - The abused person.
   - The insecure person.

5. A summary of key points to keep in mind.

Chapters 2–6 deal with each specific type of personality disorder and include:

- The *Key Points* of that particular personality disorder's behavioral style.
- Unique *Red-Flag Feelings* (reactions *for* and *against*) that each specific PDI type tries to elicit from you in order to manipulate you.
- Numerous *Picture This* examples of the behavior.
- Abundant *True-Life Adventures* illustrating in daily life how the specific PDI behaves in professional, business, and personal settings to give you possible scenarios that might occur in your life.
- How to recognize each specific type of personality disorder.
- A discussion of the basics of each particular personality disorder. This includes contrasting behaviors that can confuse you, the many ways that this personality disorder may appear to you (whether you are taken in or not), and how PDIs see themselves and want to sway you to see them (which may take you in and trap you).
- A "get to know the personality" conversation with a composite of a person with this specific personality disorder and how one would usually react.
- Typical feelings you will have in dealing with a composite of a person with this specific personality disorder.
- How to deal with each type of personality disorder. This includes what you can do and what you cannot do. We tend to repeat the same actions over and over in the hope that "this time" we will succeed. By discussing what you cannot do, *Say Goodbye to Your PDI* helps you avoid that perpetual frustration. In pointing out what you can do, *Say Goodbye to Your PDI* gives you positive steps for dealing with the PDI.
- A corrected healthier conversation with a composite of a person with this type of personality disorder.
- The types of people whom each specific personality disorder traps most.
- A summary of each particular personality disorder.

What This Book Will Do for You

This book will show you how to recognize PDIs in all walks of life. Rather than being trapped in a perpetually unhappy personal relationship or repeatedly being frustrated and angry in dealing with business or professional situations, you will become a better observer in watching unhealthy behavior unfold. By improving your perspective, you will then feel less manipulated and more in charge.

How This Book Helps You Better Recognize PDIs

First, you will be better able to spot PDIs by recognizing your own reactions to them and how the PDI uses your reactions to ensnare you. Personality disordered individuals use your feelings against you so they can control you. They may elicit guilt, envy, or even admiration from you. They then keep using these feelings to manipulate and have power over you. This book shows you the feelings which the PDI plays.

Second, you'll be better prepared for interacting with PDIs because you'll understand how the PDI behaves and wants to be perceived by you in various settings. This role is the one the PDI plays to manipulate your feelings. PDIs can play the needy waif, the seductive femme fatale, the controlling master of the universe, or Mr. Guilt to suck you into their web of manipulation.

Once you read this book, you will know what to do, and better, what *not* to do in dealing with these individuals. You will then feel more in control . . . and less *miserable*.

CHAPTER **1**

What Is a Personality Disordered Individual (PDI)?

A s in all of medicine, psychiatry has its groups of diagnoses that define certain emotional problems that people experience. Among these diagnoses are problems called *personality disorders.*

A personality disordered individual or PDI has a deeply engrained maladaptive and inflexible behavioral style that firms up around late adolescence and continues throughout adulthood. This behavior is termed a disorder because it deviates from what we, as a society, consider to be normal.

"Normal" can have many definitions. We all have our own particular and unique personality traits that make us different from other people. For the most part, we all try to cooperate with each other, bend a little when it is required, and adapt in society. Personality disordered individuals (PDIs) do not. What distinguishes them from non-PDIs is their unwavering devotion to themselves . . . at our expense. PDIs are selfish users who do not change, regardless of who they are with or what the situation is.

Personality problems appear to arise from times that go awry in our mental development. For example, the terrible twos is a normal phase of development in which a child learns how to be assertive ("It's *mine.*"). Then, as a three-year-old, the child learns to become more sociable and to share. With personality disorders, the theory is that some people, for one reason or another, get stuck in a behavioral stage that carries over into adult life. Thus, PDIs are stranded in a childhood state of mental development and never grow out of it. As adults, they continue trying to elicit responses from people around them that replicate the responses they received in their childhood and teens.

While their behavior can be curious to us for a time, generally any mature adult relationship with a PDI is impossible. Do you know anyone whose behavior reminds you of a two-year-old's? They are stubborn and dig in their heels. They are sullen, and they brood and pout and are contrary. Rarely is it fun dealing with a two-year-old in a grown-up's body.

The PDI has a behavioral disorder because he or she does not adapt, is not flexible, and behaves in a way that says, "It's all about me." PDIs, although some might at first not seem so, are self-centered and very manipulative. They use others for their own ends and rarely have empathy or concern for other people. Relationships with them (whether in a professional, business, or personal area, whether short- or long-term) are always difficult. They cause problems and misery wherever they go, which is an immediate indicator of disorder, given that most people want to avoid causing problems.

Numerous factors shape our personalities as we develop. First, there is the hereditary factor: the nervous system with which we are born. Our nervous system determines how we sense our world, whether we filter things out or become overstimulated by them. Next comes our environment. Is it kind, gentle, and giving, or rough, demanding, and cruel?

As we grow both mentally and physically, we pass through stages in which we are supposed to learn new ways of adapting to life so that when we reach adulthood we are prepared to function in a mature way. In this context, "mature" means having the ability to cope with life with minimal stress and to be happy.

Our personality—our temperament, our style, our beliefs, our morals, and our philosophy of life—defines who we are. Our personality contributes to what we believe about life and people, and how each day we behave toward others and ourselves. How you behave comes from what you believe inside and defines who you are.

Since PDIs are basically still children in their mental development, they are afraid of "normal" adult relationships—with their ups and downs, the possibility of being hurt, and being asked to give, compromise, or share. They just do not have the mental equipment for it. Rather than participate in that experience, PDIs need to keep you under their control in a relationship that is *solely on their terms*. They see you in a certain light that is never good. PDIs treat you badly, and when you express some dissatisfaction, they see it as criticism and as your being hurtful, not constructive. Since people hurt (and cannot be trusted), PDIs then justify their continued aberrant behavior because of their self-centered belief that the world (you and I) is there for their own singular use.

Although psychiatrists presently identify a total of ten distinct and unique personality disorders, this book concentrates primarily on the five we most frequently encounter and who cause the most misery for us because of their very intrusive behaviors.

While it is no longer considered a distinct personality disorder, I have included in this list the passive-aggressive personality disorder because people with this behavior appear so frequently in our daily lives and can be so controlling.

These personality problems are distinguished by how each PDI relates to and controls people. In short, each is defined by the particular style the PDI uses to manipulate you. Most PDIs need to have you constantly close to them in their need to control you. These particular PDIs are very social and dramatic people who need to control others and thus must have that interaction.

There are two categories of PDIs separated by their behavioral styles. In the first category are *the blamers,* who are PDIs who provoke and control you with guilt. These people have passive-aggressive personality disorder. They are negative and attempt to push the blame for their problems on everyone else. This is Mr. Negative—the two-year-old in a grown-up's body.

The second category contains the *dramatic and erratic* PDIs who overwhelm and control you with the power of their personality. In this group of four, we find:

- The *seductress,* who is emotional and attention-seeking. This is the histrionic PDI.
- The *smooth operator,* who charms, beguiles, and captivates you, but who is actually quite cold inside. This PDI displays the antisocial personality disorder.
- The *intense, demanding, extreme, and unstable* PDI, who has the borderline personality disorder. Think *Fatal Attraction.*
- The *egotistic and pompous,* who exist to be adored and admired. These characteristics describe the narcissistic personality disorder.

Remember ──

PDIs are rigid and inflexible in their behavior. They believe that you adapt to them. They do not adapt to you.

──

HOW A PDI BEHAVES

PDIs' behaviors can be charming, infuriating, alluring, endearing, stimulating, awe-inspiring, loathsome, entrancing, avoidable, strange, perplexing, a curiosity, or a pain in the neck. They play a gamut of roles to pique your interest and seduce you into their world—the world of "me." With several of the specific personality disorders, a pleasant and stimulating time with the PDI can occur . . . before the misery begins. PDIs are certainly challenging and high-maintenance. They are *always* memorable.

PDIs have their own agenda of what they need psychologically—for example, attention, domination, adoration, control, avoidance, dependency—depending on the period of emotional maturation in which they stalled. They have developed a time-tested way to behave, designed to suck you into dealing with them so they can get the attention they feel they need. They are often successful—since they are such good manipulators—in getting what they feel they need, e.g., attention from you or power over you. The PDI throws out the line and sees what new victim bites.

For example, an individual with the histrionic personality disorder goes fishing with her seductiveness as the lure while feigning neediness so a white knight will help her. The person with passive-aggressive personality disorder baits others with guilt and uses that to manipulate.

In a situation involving interaction with a professional, the PDI's goal can move beyond attention or power to something more concrete, such as medication from a doctor, extrication from legal matters from a lawyer, or permission from a social worker to do some desired action. Whatever they are looking to get from you, PDI's will still use their basic exploitative behaviors to get to their ends.

In business, PDIs always behave for their own personal ends and will use others only for their own advancement.

PDIs bring the most misery to personal relationships. In these situations, PDIs can be incredibly selfish, self-centered, and demanding.

Remember

You can identify PDIs because they behave repeatedly in a way to provoke you in some manner (a pleasant or not-so-pleasant one) and get a rise out of you. They will use your reaction to manipulate you.

HOW PDIS AFFECT YOU

When we interact with each other, we may feel various emotions. We might feel pleased if we get our way with something or frustrated if we do not. We might feel good in being praised. We might be provocative in trying to elicit a response. We may do something in anger because another person hurt us. We all vary in our behaviors and generally work at achieving harmony and fairness with each other.

In contrast, the PDI's manipulative behavior is not confined to specific instances. PDIs *always* have some ulterior motive in mind, with their desired end being to provoke you (for example, by inspiring guilt, admiration, or sexual arousal), and then to use this feeling against you. PDIs at first behave by fishing to see what feeling they can elicit from you and then using it against you.

The important and frequently hard part is to recognize their behavior and to prevent getting ensnared in their behavioral style. Once we are hooked, the misery begins and does not change.

A license plate holder reads, "I drive this way to piss you off." What kind of feeling does this simple, short sentence proclaimed on the frame of someone's license plate bring out in you? Anger? *What a jerk,* maybe. It is provocative, is it not? More to the point, this license plate offers just the kind of action that a person with passive-aggressive personality disorder would do. Here is what basically happens:

• He takes some action, such as cutting you off while driving.

- You respond, asking him if he knew what he was doing. Perhaps you swear, silently fume, or accept your powerless fate . . . but the guy still irked you.
- He responds, asking why you're so sensitive—perhaps giving you a hand gesture or deliberately driving badly, yet still getting away with his behavior.
- You feel bad—maybe angry or guilty for having said or thought something.

This simple little scenario shows how the PDI works to get a rise out of you. Even though the encounter is short, it still leaves us feeling bad, used, and manipulated. The more enduring situations leave us miserable.

By the time they've reached adulthood, PDIs have been acting in their particular way for a long time and have typically become very good at what they do. Each specific type of PDI works to evoke one particular feeling in you (e.g., guilt, lust, anger) and to do it consistently. Ever walk away from a conversation with someone and think, *Whenever I talk with him, I come away feeling guilty about something,* or *What does that guy do to always get me angry?* The level of interaction does not change. However, the PDI has a vast portfolio of ways to get at you. The PDI fisherman or -woman has many lures. He or she will get a rise out of you.

Remember ─────────────────────────────

The PDI's behavior is focused on provoking a rise out of you that is then used to control you.

HOW YOU GET TRAPPED AND MANIPULATED BY A PDI'S BEHAVIOR

The PDI's crafty behavior traps and manipulates you. You get suckered. Nobody ever feels good when that happens. Hopefully, we let go of the temporary situations, although they do not contribute to having a good day. The more recurring miserable situations in our daily lives are the ones that certainly cause the most duress.

Why does a PDI get a reaction from you? Because you are human. How do you get trapped? Because you are human.

PDIs thrive on the reactions of non–personality-disordered *normal* human beings who respond to provocative words and behaviors. PDIs expect some recognition or some validation of what they are saying. Normal human beings do not expect their words to be turned back on them as PDIs do. We feel frustrated, angry, and confused; we might even back off and think that we are at fault. Normal human beings also expect, with further discussion, to work the situation out and find some middle ground. This *never* happens with a PDI.

PDIs always turn things back on you and keep you confused or angry, or whatever feeling they use to manipulate. If you think you know a PDI, think about it. You never get a sense of being heard with that person, nor do you ever have a sense of validation for what you are feeling. It is always their way. (If you do think you are being heard, they are only playing you.)

A PDI's behavior traps us in one of two main ways: either we react by giving in to the PDI's way of seeing things—leading to our feeling power-less—or we react against the PDI by continuing to fight to be heard—which will never happen, so we still feel frustrated and powerless. Throughout this book, we identify these reactions as the *red-flag feelings* described with each specific personality disorder. We should keep in mind throughout that our sense of powerless results in misery time and time again.

In discussing the specific personality disorders, you'll learn that some PDIs manipulate with personal charm, daring deeds done to impress, sexual intimations, or a neediness designed to bring out parenting or the rescuer in us. At first, we may be easily confounded by these reactions because the feeling evoked is not disagreeable but rather pleasant. But the pleasant feeling quickly gives way to the PDI's purpose, which is using you. Essentially, you are just more pleasantly trapped into a state of misery.

Remember

PDIs trap you by using your normal human behavior and responses against you. You expect one response, and they surprise you with another.

WHY YOU STAY TRAPPED

If I am so miserable, why would I stay trapped in such a situation?

Think of how a salesperson who wants you to buy something keeps you coming back to a store. They do it with the lure, the promise, and the hook. Being human, we tend to fall for these things.

PDIs use the emotional hook. If we are angry with them, they keep us coming back for satisfaction. If they succeed in making us feel guilty, they have us coming back for absolution. If we think they need us, we keep coming back to help. If they promise great things (money, advancement), we keep coming back to get them.

This type of relationship takes place in all aspects of life. A professional might be complimented into bending rules; a businessperson entranced by promises of advancement doesn't comprehend or overlooks how much he or she is used; a personal relationship might be controlled by guilt. We stay trapped because we humanly believe there is something beyond what is actually happening. We believe that other humans do not act this way and that "things can be worked out." We refuse to accept that another person may be using us, or we blame ourselves because things are not going better. We think, *It must be me. Maybe if I work it a little more. . . .* In a professional or business setting, we may think we are too smart to be used. We stay trapped because we fail to accept that PDIs use people, plain and simple. We can only accept blame if we allow it to continue.

Remember ———————————————————————

PDIs want to keep you confused and on the ropes indefinitely. By doing this, they can keep using you forever.

HOW TO RECOGNIZE A PDI
SO YOU WILL NOT GET TRAPPED

As you should see by now, being aware of your emotional response to the PDI is crucial. The essential but frequently difficult thing is to identify your feelings when you are with the PDI. Once you see how the PDI operates and how you feel, you can prevent yourself from becoming ensnared in the PDI's trap and feeling the recurring unpleasantness that takes place. Once we are hooked, the misery goes on forever. By keeping you off balance, the PDI seeks to control and manipulate you for his or her own ends. The PDI's main goal is to get and keep you on the defensive or emotionally control you in some way to use you.

First, you need to recognize the PDI by seeing his or her pattern of behavior as well as your own repeated responses. Frequently, identifying your own pattern is difficult because you have been doing it for so long. It is hard (and humbling) to step back and say, "How could I have been so dumb for so long?" What you need is a better perspective, to view the PDI's behavior as objectively as possible. What does he or she do to get you going? What are the mannerisms? What does he or she say? What is he or she implying? How does he or she dress? Most important, how does he or she try to make you feel?

Does the PDI praise, promise, or try to impress you? Does the PDI try to intimidate or challenge you? Is she seductive, or is she needy? Is he strange, and does he put you off but somehow still engage you?

Once you identify the recurring pattern, you must become an objective observer rather than a participant. You must begin to view the interaction like watching a movie. You must learn to watch the moves of the PDI, how he or she adapts and changes if you do not at first respond as he or she wishes. Initially, you will find yourself able to do this, but you may still succumb. Remember, the PDI is an expert at this, while you're just learning.

Eventually, you will become more adept at recognizing the behavior, and you will stop feeling so used or manipulated. You will feel more in control of the situation, more confident, and ultimately less miserable.

Remember

The first and most important guide in dealing with a PDI is to monitor your feelings and responses.

THE PRIME THINGS TO REMEMBER WHEN DEALING WITH PDIS

PDIs have their own agenda of emotional needs that come first with them. Whether you think you know this agenda or not, you must remember that, whatever you do, you can never meet the PDI's psychological needs, even if you think you understand him or her. If you are a professional, you may think you have the upper hand since they are coming to see you for your wisdom. *Forget it!* In business, you might think that you can handle a PDI by talking about the company, the people, even power and prestige. *Forget it!* PDIs have their own agenda.

Especially in personal relationships, if you believe you can help or change them, you are doomed. The needs of PDIs are so profound that no mortal could ever hope to fulfill them . . . or even hope to help them understand their behavior. A PDI may in some cases appear to be craving closeness and understanding, but, in truth, that is the furthest thing from the PDI's mind. PDIs have expectations like "Never criticize me," "Always be there," "Give me all of your attention," "Take all my hurt away," "Don't get close," "You are here to serve only me," and "Always treat me as extra special."

These expectations are so unrealistic that anyone in any form of a relationship with a PDI is condemned to failure. If you try to help, you will never live up to their expectations, no matter what you do. If you confront them, you become hurtful, a betrayer who cannot be trusted. Either way, if you try to tolerate them or if you confront them with their unrealistic demands, you are frustrated and miserable. You think you can reason with them or that you can work things out. You might even get angry and demand to be heard, but this will never happen.

Remember ───

You will not be able to help or change a PDI's behavior, but you can certainly change yours.

───

As you read through this book, you will identify with various personality traits described in the disorders. We all grow up with some of these traits.

The big difference is that most of us do not find ourselves in difficulties because of this behavior. We recognize it as a way we do not want to be, try to change it, and hopefully apologize to anyone we may have bothered. We are not stuck in a persisting, immature way of behaving, but PDIs are. PDIs do things in a certain way, with their behavior guaranteed to elicit a definite, repeated emotional response from us. They then use this response to manipulate us.

Having a sense of control over our own lives is extremely important in dealing with PDIs. When we are manipulated and our sense of control is wrested away from us repeatedly, we become distraught, confused, demoralized, depressed . . . and miserable.

THE BASICS ABOUT PDIS

When you find yourself in or facing a relationship with a PDI, you must keep the following facts in mind:

- **They do not change.** They have a rigid and enduring way of behaving that unerringly gets them into difficulties over and over again. Ironically, others' reactions to their behavior only reinforce the behavior.
- **They will *repeatedly* try to provoke you (in a good or bad way).** They seek to bring out a particular emotion that they can then use against you.
- **They trap you by using your feelings against you.**
- **They *always* blame others.** You respond in a normal way, and quickly you are being manipulated. Unfortunately, since they do not see things as most of us do, PDIs do not perceive the problem as their own and invariably blame others. If confronted with troublesome behavior—whether at work, seeking professional help, or at home or with others—PDIs do not try to understand what they are doing and change, but, in fact, their behavior usually worsens.
- **They will fool you.** A person with a personality disorder can still be successful in terms of notoriety, success, money, or employment. PDIs can be accomplished businesspeople, entrepreneurs, movie stars, superheroes, or highly respected individuals. Having a personality disorder simply means that they are difficult to live and deal with in terms of how

they behave with us common folk. They make us miserable. They can string you along for years while you kid yourself that they are trying . . . but things never improve.

- **You cannot change them.** As we discuss through this book how to deal with PDIs, keep in mind that their habits developed far back in their lives and are fixed. If a PDI is fairly bright, he or she may smarten up. Perhaps when they see that they are neither controlling people nor winning friends and influencing people by one way of behaving, they adapt. The PDI may appear to change, but what really is happening is that he or she is only outwardly making some adjustments. PDIs can shift gears to another method of manipulation and control. Their goal is still to get what they need, and it has nothing to do with you or understanding your side. If you think they are changing, think again.

- **They are never wrong.** They are in denial about any problems they may have. They always have excuses, *never* saying they are sorry, and their behavior worsens when they are confronted with it. In a PDI's mind, *you* are expected to change. *You* are to be controlled, not them.

- **They are selfish and self-centered.** It is *all* about them.

WHAT YOU CAN DO

Assess how the person makes you feel each time you deal with the PDI. You may feel guilty, bedazzled, angry, in awe, helpless, frustrated, inadequate, defensive, or wanting to rescue the poor thing (particularly true for professionals). That feeling you repeatedly experience is the key to identifying the problem and will help you immensely in deciding your moves.

Remember ———————————————————

Check out your misery level. Look at how your feelings make you respond to the PDI's behavior. Your responses are likely to be well intentioned, but they do not seem to work because of the PDI's manipulating ways and your responses being part of the PDI's plan, not yours.

Remember ───

The most important point to bear in mind as you deal with a PDI is as follows: If it does not work, do not keep doing it!

───

WHAT TYPES OF PEOPLE ARE MOST TRAPPED BY PDIS?

PDIs have ensnared every one of us at one time or another in our lives. They succeed at this because PDIs are very good at what they do: manipulating others.

They connive, lie, flatter, seduce, guiltify, sweet-talk, promise, or otherwise exploit us. After our experience with them, we are usually left saying to ourselves, "I should've done this" or "I should've said that," because we did not come out of the encounter feeling good about what happened.

Since PDIs make us miserable, "Why," you may ask, "do any of us stay in a relationship with them for any longer than we have to?" That is part of the shrewdness of PDIs. By their behavior, they trap us into believing that we are locked into a relationship and that we are helpless in thinking otherwise. As we are tricked, we also trick ourselves. We tragically con ourselves with many excuses.

In a professional setting, you might say, "It's my job," or "I'm here to help (or advise or consult with) people with problems, that's why they come to me." Or you might simply say to yourself, "I can put up with this because the money is good." Some misguided professionals see themselves as rescuers (see below in the categories of those who stay), whose role in life is to save others from their problems. Since PDIs never change, tolerating their misery-generating behavior becomes fruitless, frustrating, and foul, even if the money is good. Why try to continue to professionally help someone who does not listen or want to change?

In business, you might endure a degree of misery as you tell yourself that you are "paying your dues." For example, if you are a student, trainee, apprentice, or a business associate, or in some position where you will gain training, knowledge, prestige, or a "golden" experience to put on your resume—and the misery is time-limited—then it becomes "acceptable" . . . as long as you are getting out at some future time. Here, there is a tradeoff. However, the other excuses—"I can't find anything else," "He'll hurt me professionally if I leave," "The job gives me security," "Where will I go?" or "You can't beat the money"—are all groundless reasons to maintain a wretched existence.

In our personal lives, why we continue to invest ourselves in losing relationships that make us miserable is like trying to answer why people fall in love. Wise people have written myriads of sage words and singers have sung countless songs about heartache, yet the mystery endures of why we stay in an unhappy relationship.

Having written that, I shall attempt to give you some reasons that someone who would be considered a rational, sensible, and caring person continues to suffer in professional, business, or personal relationships that daily cause them woe.

Remember

We all have some of the following traits, more or less. The danger is when these traits so influence our behavior that we are more doomed to get into a miserable state and to stay there.

These are the various categories of individuals who are more prone to be trapped and to allow themselves to stay in miserable situations with PDIs:

The Caring Person

This person has had a fairly healthy upbringing where people treated each other with love and respect. These types of people have had the experience of working things out in relationships. In growing up, they have seen conflicts between their parents, but have also seen the problems resolved with fairness and the desire to make things right. As they grew up, they have had their own issues with brothers, sisters, friends, and lovers, and have learned that talking things out can solve interpersonal issues. They have seen that a relationship needs constant work from both parties. From his or her life experience, this type of person has come to expect a give-and-take in a relationship where compromise is sometimes necessary. When this does not happen (for example, because the other party has a personality disorder), the caring person is bewildered and confused. Because these types of individuals are emotionally strong and have had healthy relationships with others, this type of experience initially stymies them. They find it perplexing that another person who professes to love them (or who wants to help or wants to work cohesively) continues to make them miserable and behave opposite to what a healthy relationship should be. He or she wonders, *What's going on here? Things aren't going like they usually do for me in relationships. Am I missing something?* Since these types of people are caring and concerned, they try harder to make things work out. They are accustomed to solving these problems and begin to blame themselves if problems persist.

However, because these people are sensible and confident, they do not stay too long in the relationship. Professionals treating, counseling, or advising a PDI often terminate with uncooperative clients; people in business transfer to another department, make a move within the company, or find another job.

These individuals usually come to grips with the fact that they have tried their best to make the relationship work. Sometimes, it may take them a few months or even a few years, but they eventually resolve the self-blame and go on with their lives. Sometimes, they seek short-term counseling to confirm their instincts that it is not always two parties who cause a relationship to founder. Relationships with PDIs always go downhill with the PDI never taking any blame.

The Rescuer

The rescuer is a variant of the caring person, but the rescuer takes the relationship to another level. Rescuers are attracted to needy persons, people who appear to have various difficulties that beckon to someone to help out. Rescuers are problem-solvers and fancy themselves as being the ones who will champion the needy with whatever troubles they may have. Another role for the rescuer is the white knight or the nurse. They are savior or caretaker types who will make all the bad stuff go away. Rescuers frequently were the responsible person in their family and are carrying on this family role into adulthood.

When they were growing up, some unhappy event in their family life may have occurred—like a parent's suicide, a sibling dying, or chronic illness in a loved one—but it was something over which they, as a child, had no control. Now as adults they see themselves as trying to make things right. In their rescuing roles, these individuals try to undo the powerlessness and unhappiness they experienced as children.

Many advisory or therapeutic professionals fall into this category. They have a particular expertise and want to help others out while they make a living.

Unfortunately, some PDIs use the "I'm lost and needy" ploy to entice you and then exploit your need to help. (See the sections later in this book on histrionic and borderline personality disorders.)

PDIs can repeatedly convey a profound illusion of needing (when actually they are controlling) you and recurrently entrap you and perpetuate the relationship, whatever type it may be—professional, business, or personal.

If you as the rescuer do not catch on early in the relationship that you cannot be responsible for another person's happiness or success, you will stay on with some fantasy (kindled by the PDI) that you will make things better. You must keep a perspective of what you can and cannot do. If you do not, PDIs will control and use you. Since they really do not want anyone rescuing them, you will just stay frustrated and wretched.

The Guilty One

If anything is amiss, these folks blame themselves first. Since PDIs accept no blame for their actions, the guilty person is the perfect individual for the PDI to trap and exploit (see later sections on passive-aggressive and compulsive personality disorders). Guilty people grew up in an environment where their parents and others used guilt as a potent manipulating force. One of the prominent ways the family operated was to never to take responsibility for something going wrong and to guiltify something or someone else for their troubles.

As guilty ones grew up, they would hear things like "I got fired because the boss was jealous of me (not because I was lazy)," or "If you didn't nag me so much, maybe I wouldn't have to drink." In these families, it was very easy to blame the child for the woes of the parent(s), with the child hearing things like, "You know it's your fault that I'm unhappy. I never wanted you in the first place." Think about being a guileless and trusting child and hearing this over and over. The more sensitive the child is, the more devastating and influencing these statements are.

Not surprisingly, guilty people grow up with a sense that something wrong is their fault. Later in life, they invariably fall into a relationship with someone like a PDI, who expertly uses the guilt to keep this person under his or her thumb. Because these individuals have been programmed into believing they are always to blame, they are doomed to stay in this type of relationship indefinitely, unless, at some point, the light bulb goes on in their heads and they begin to think differently.

You might think that this type of person could meet someone nice who tries to compliment them and focus on the good points. Unfortunately, this type of relationship does not last long, because the forever-guilty person thinks one of two things: either "I know I'm no good, so this person is lying to me to use me," or "This person really doesn't know me. I don't deserve someone this nice."

The Giver

These people are somewhat like the guilty person, only they focus less on their guilt (although it is there) and more on doing for others. These are the people-pleasers. Givers stuff their own needs and wants and see their role as being a help to others. They do not presume to be able to rescue. They are simply there to make others' lives better. Givers never raise their voices, nor do they speak out for themselves or their needs. They were taught the "proper" way to act, which excludes being assertive and thinking about oneself. That would be selfish. No self-respecting PDI could turn away this type of person, so ripe for exploitation (see later sections on the passive-aggressive and antisocial personality disorders). Givers not infrequently have much anger held deep inside them, for having to put their wishes aside for so long. However, since anger is not "proper," they can never deal with it. This is another ideal situation for PDIs, who can avoid any confrontation for their outrageous behaviors.

The Abused Person

Verbal bullying and threats ("Keep that up and I'll take you out into the swamp and leave you alone to die"), sexual abuse ("If you tell anyone about this, I'll hurt you"), or physical intimidation or abuse ("If you do that again, I'll beat you") filled many maltreated individuals' family lives.

Abused people are responsible, compliant, cooperative, nonconfrontational, passive, avoidant, and pleasant (at least on the outside). They believe, "Don't do anything, and nothing will happen to you. Go with the flow (because you may be hurt some way if you don't)."

PDIs who can bully or intimidate (see later sections on narcissistic, antisocial, and passive-aggressive personality disorders) easily manipulate abused people. Mistreated individuals fall into a thought pattern that abuse is a way of life in relationships with others. They have adopted the attitude that nothing really works to change things, so they passively accept their plight. They go through life accepting whatever is given them. They believe that "I am powerless to do much about anything." Their goal each day is to minimize how much abuse they receive rather than to see abuse as inappropriate and unacceptable. As a result, they unwittingly allow misery and abusive people into their lives.

The Insecure Person

Insecure people can fall into all of the above categories, but they may not have had significant mistreatment in one form or another as they grew up. These are the average people among us who are not too confident and not too assertive. Insecure individuals lack firm convictions about themselves and their rights. They may not be too self-reliant or independent, and they rely on others for advice and direction. PDIs thrive on the insecure. They play on the lack of confidence and/or they promise security.

Women may suffer from the "I need someone to lean on" syndrome, or worse, the "What would happen to me if someone isn't around" syndrome (all PDIs trap these people). Self-doubting men fall prey more to the narcissistic personality individual who exploits feelings of inadequacy.

Insecure people fall into the trap of believing that they cannot exist by themselves and really need a relationship. No matter how miserable they are, they keep thinking, "At least I'm not alone." It is not difficult to predict that this type of man or woman can also get into a relationship where they feel manipulated and used, but, because of their fears and insecurities, they see no way out. If they are sensitive to the judgment of others ("What will my family think?"), they are further stuck.

A typical person who fits this mold is one who's middle-aged or older. They feel very insecure in extricating themselves from an abysmal relationship that has been part of their lives for years. At an older age, they wonder, "What can I do? Where will I go?" They have been in the relationship so long that there appears to be no other alternatives but to stay and be stuck.

Why do human beings continue to endure miserable relationships? PDIs use our insecurities, doubts, vanities, fantasies, frustrations, or whatever else they see as a hook to exploit us and keep us around (or not around, in some cases where the PDI wants us at a distance). Those who tolerate a relationship in which they are constantly manipulated have a tremendous off-base concept of what a relationship should be. Relationships in any sphere of life—professional, personal, or business-related—should be based on mutual respect, compromise, and cooperation, not on exploitation, manipulation, self-concern, and blamelessness, which occur with a PDI.

The goal of this book is to help you recognize how PDIs trap you into a miserable situation and show you what you can do about it. Once you are more empowered by a better perspective and use the tools in this book to deal with the PDI, you will have a more solid understanding of what a relationship should be. You will be less likely to be used . . . and less likely to be miserable.

Sadly, we can be more secure (but not happy) in denying, avoiding, rationalizing, or focusing on other things as causes for our misery than to face up to the real issues and make changes. Many times people will tell me they are confused about their problems. However, being confused often feels more comfortable than the anxiety that might result from attempting to change. It takes a great deal of courage and support to begin to look at one's own beliefs, to trust in others (who have a healthier view of life), and to begin to make changes.

Remember ————————————————————————

Personality disordered individuals do not change.

SUMMARY

The material that we have covered so far, which provides a foundation for our discussions of individual personality disorders, can be summarized as follows. In all aspects of life, professional, business, and personal:

- PDIs make you miserable.
- PDIs act in a way to get a reaction from you.
- PDIs use that reaction to trap you into dealing with them in a specific way (their way).
- PDIs never change, and they are never wrong.
- To begin to lessen your misery, you must identify how PDIs make you feel.
- You must change your reactions to the PDI to be happier.

CHAPTER 2

The Blamers: Passive-Aggressive Personality Disorder (PA)

Mr. or Ms. Negative, the Two-Year-Old in a Grown-Up's Body, the Whiner

"Now what are you complaining about?"

K*ey Point:* Passive-aggressive personality disorder (PA for short) has been termed the most miserable personality disorder. Nicknames for a person with PA might be the Complainer, Joe Gloom, Dreary Dan, or Ms. Grumble. These people have the most negative type of personality you will encounter. PAs thrive on trapping you in situations in which everything you do or say is wrong. Whenever you deal with a PA, you are immediately put in a position of having to explain yourself or to justify something. You then feel guilty and defensive, or you feel angry and defensive. Either way, the PA has elicited a rise out of you and uses it to control you, seeking to make you as miserable as he or she is.

The PA needs to be miserable to maintain the self-image of being a forlorn victim of life. A PA's controlling behavior manipulates you into feeding that self-image. Either you are agreeing with the PA about your being guilty for your "wrongful" actions, or you are reacting angrily to the PA, confirming that you are "hurtful."

A PA's particular traits are being negative, oppositional, faultfinding, undermining, and always arguing about something. The term *passive-aggressive* comes from the PA's indirect whining and complaining, which is, in fact, very aggressive in provoking feelings.

Red-Flag Feelings in You

Guilt (defensiveness)

Anger

Picture This

Who Are the PAs You Might See?

An individual is driving in front of you on a two-lane road and going twenty miles per hour in a forty-five-mile-per-hour zone. You finally get beside him at a light and glare. He says, "What the hell's wrong with you?"

Think of the fellow at the theater who has his legs out in the aisle, making it impossible for you to pass. He moans and groans, sighs, and makes a big deal out of having to move because of the inconvenience you are causing him.

Remember ————————————————————————————

The PA lives to provoke you. This is how it works: he goads you, you respond.

———————————————————————————————————————

You are in a bar and a fellow comes up and asks if he can buy you a drink. You decline, and he says, "I guess I'm not good enough for you." Or you pay for your drink with cash, and he says, "It must be nice to be rich." In these instances, he is baiting you as he seeks some response where he can put you in the wrong.

You hire a woman to do some work for you. She keeps you waiting long beyond the time she was supposed to show up. When she finally arrives, you mention the time. She says, "I'm here now. Are you going to waste my time complaining?" When she does a poor job (and she will) and you comment on it, she says, "I don't need this! I don't see any problem. If I knew you were going to be so picky, I wouldn't have taken this lousy job." Then she asks you to pay her.

Remember ————————————————————————————

PAs are very contrary, demeaning, and insulting. Unless you agree with them, everything is an argument.

———————————————————————————————————————

Picture This

Professional Life

In a business or professional setting, the PA often exhibits the following behavior:

- Always late for appointments.
- Questions any and all of your comments, suggestions, or recommendations.
- Gets indignant over your advice.
- Seems to cooperate but then undermines or sabotages anything you suggest ("I couldn't do that because . . .").

If they pay their bill, these individuals pay late and make you work to collect your fee ("You're rich enough already. Besides, you didn't do anything for me anyway"). The PA can and will take up much of the appointment time talking about:

- His sorry situation.
- His woes.
- His being misunderstood.
- His good intentions that are so misinterpreted.
- His victimization by a cruel and uncaring world (which includes you).

Whatever your professional capacity, as long as you just listen, you are still okay. But if you question, challenge, or confront the PA's way of seeing things (which you would likely do in your role as the professional)—for example, by saying, "Did you ever think that you might be the one at fault here?" or "Do you think you might have some part to play in your problems?"—you become the bad guy for not understanding him.

The PA has no inkling of how this negativity, whining, and faultfinding affect others. As a client or patient, a PA keeps "forgetting" to send you the documents or files you need while asking you to explain *everything* and attacking your credibility ("What's your background? Are you experienced? How can you understand what I'm going through?"), especially when you begin to ask probing questions.

If you are a professional, people seek you out for your expertise in some area. You are accustomed to giving direction, treatment, advice, or counsel, and the person who is consulting you usually follows that counsel because he or she is paying for it. Not so with PAs. They may seem to be seeking your help, but they will undermine and sabotage your plans to lend a hand. At times, PAs may seem willing to accept your recommendations, yet they never follow through. PAs can be extremely frustrating, irritating, and angering, and they are adept at provoking guilt in you. You can wind up thinking things like, *What am I not doing right? Why can't I get through to this guy?*

A doctor told me about a patient who had severe emphysema but still smoked. The patient complained to the doctor how he felt tricked by him into taking a test to assess his lungs. The patient said, "You SOB! You deliberately embarrassed me with that test to show I had lung problems. If you think I'll stop smoking now, you're crazy. That's no way to practice medicine. You know nothing about treating people."

Remember

PAs are oppositional by nature. Even though they seem to want to seek out your help, to them you are an authority figure against whom they must rebel.

Another example of PA behavior would be the client who leaves you an urgent message to call him, but is then unavailable. After many tries, you get him on the phone. His first comment is, "Sorry to pull you away from your golf game." He is playing you into feeling confused and on the defensive— as if you should apologize for not returning his call sooner—even though he was the one who was difficult to reach.

Remember

Relieve yourself of any notion that PAs want specific help from you, other than for you to agree with them.

Passive-aggressive people rarely seek you out professionally on their own. If they do, it is to complain, whine, accuse, and complain some more to get your sympathy and confirm their belief that all others are hurtful. PAs usually consult with you out of pressure from some outside force: legal entanglements, partners or spouses, something medical (a physical ailment that might impede their controlling style), or job problems. Whatever the motivation, PAs see it as their being singled out and treated unfairly by uncaring others.

The PA will be late for the appointment that he or she probably did not want in the first place. Initially, he or she may be grumpy or extremely personable. Either way, you will have a tough time pulling out from the PA the real reason that he or she is seeking your services. You will never get the whole story. If you do not have much background information from another source and only hear the PA's side of the story, you may be astounded to hear how badly the PA is being mistreated, misunderstood, or victimized in one form or another. The PA will deny any responsibility for the problems and will always blame others. You'll have a picture of an innocent human in the uncaring world of the haves and have-nots, and your PA is most certainly a have-not.

If you already have some background information, you will be awed by the disparity between what others report and what the PA tells you. PAs will question anything and everything you suggest, letting you know what independent thinkers they are (the eagle soaring over the turkeys) and the scorn they have for authority (you) and the more fortunate (also you).

Remember

Everything negative that a PA says about others may (and probably will) be said about you. As soon as you question anything about PAs or what they are saying, you become the opposition.

True Life

True-Life Adventure 1:
Righteous Rich and the Attorney

Rich played loud music through the night and let his dogs outside bark unendingly. He alienated most of his neighbors who tried repeatedly to talk with him but found him angry, defiant, and unreasonable. They finally called the police, who also found Rich to have an attitude problem. They arrested him for disturbing the peace and resisting an officer. Rich maintained that he was only exercising his rights as an American to do what he wanted on his property.

With much complaining, Rich consulted an attorney. During the appointment, Rich ranted on about his troublemaking and vengeful neighbors, the Nazi cops, the legal system, sleazeball lawyers and their overcharging, crooked judges, his rights as an American, and so on.

After many minutes of listening to Rich's rantings, the lawyer expressed his confusion and asked what his point was. Rich said, "This isn't about you, it's about me! What do *you* know? You cannot understand. Why are you picking on me? I came to see you for help, not criticism."

Remember ──────────────────────────────────

PAs seethe with scornful resentment at any authority—even though they may be seeking help.

───

True Life

True-Life Adventure 2:
Fractious Frank and Dr. Bob

Frank was suing a local corporation for discrimination against him. Frank believed that the company did not understand his alleged psychiatric problems and thus put undue stress on him. Frank's company requested that he consult with Dr. Bob, a psychiatrist, to allow him to evaluate the extent of Frank's psychiatric problems.

Frank was early for his appointment, but stayed in the parking lot and came late into the office. After tracking mud in from the outside, Frank let Dr. Bob know what an imposition it was for him to be there. Frank then thanked Dr. Bob for taking time away from treating neurotic housewives to see him.

Frank whined and complained about how he was set up by the callous and inconsiderate "bastard manager" of the large corporation where he had worked. He had no idea how one of his tools was left in the jet engine he was working on and ruined its functioning. Sure, in another incident he had destroyed some company property, but it was that "SOB boss" who had surprised him with the false accusation of sexual harassment and who made him get angry enough to do that damage. Besides, the female employee who filed the complaint made him say something sexual because of her behavior and how she looked. "Anyway," said Frank, "the company has lots of money, and I deserve some of it. They were just looking for things to get me. It's not my fault they never appreciated what I did for them."

Frank continued, "Doc, you don't know what it's like to work hard, to have a boss, to put up with the daily grind, or to have an ungrateful wife. You've got it easy, like the stinking lawyers the company bought to get me. All I wanted to do was to take care of my family and be treated fairly, but people always had it in for me. I'm under a lot of stress."

Dr. Bob sat and listened to a guy who saw himself as perpetually wounded and victimized by insensitive forces that never understood him. Frank was contemptuous, spiteful, dissatisfied, sullen, and provocative. He resented everything and everyone around him, including the doctor. No one appreciated him. Frank told Dr. Bob that he was so nervous before his 9 AM appointment that he had two beers to calm him. "Do you blame me, Doc?"

Dr. Bob, always trying to be the understanding psychiatrist, tried to be sensitive to Frank's situation. Dr. Bob felt guilty for being initially angry at Frank's challenging behavior and not seeing Frank's side of things.

Remember ─────────────────────────────────

The PA is always the victim of an uncaring world. You are unfair and hurtful if you think otherwise.

───

True Life

True-Life Adventure 3:
Sulky Sam and Mary, the Social Worker

Sam made an appointment to speak with Mary, a social worker. Sam's wife had gone to Mary for counseling regarding increasing anxiety and depression. Early in the treatment, Mary realized that Sam's wife was in a terrible marriage with a verbally abusive and guilt-inspiring man. Mary addressed her therapy at helping the wife be more confident and assertive.

Sam made the appointment ostensibly to give Mary more information. Sam's information was essentially that his wife was an unreasonable harpy who would not do things right in the marriage. Sam went on about the many faults of his wife and his own goodness in putting up with her.

Sam turned his attention to Mary. He was scornful of her treatment and said, "Since coming to you, things are worse at home. Whatever you're telling her, it's all wrong." Mary smiled inwardly since she knew that Sam's wife was being more confrontational with this bully and certainly upsetting his system of control by intimidation and guilt. As Sam left he told Mary, "With all of your supposed training, you have no idea what you're doing. You've failed miserably in helping my wife."

Remember

The PA will attack your professionalism in some way either to bring out guilt ("Hmmm, maybe I have been wrong about this guy") or anger so you will act in a punitive or harsh way.

Picture This

Business Life

In the business setting, PAs will sabotage and undermine projects. Their characteristics are as follows:

- They are obstructive and oppositional and generally bring out the worst in fellow employees.
- They are always late to work or with work.
- Their excuse for poor performance is always someone else's inadequacy.
- They see only the gloomy side and pull morale down.
- They are the faultfinders on any project, plan, or person.
- They make you watch your back.

True Life

True-Life Adventure 1:
John the Jerk and Pat

John is Pat's boss. He abruptly schedules a meeting with her and some other coworkers but gives no reason for it. One of three scenarios would be typical for a PA in this situation:

1. John arrives thirty minutes late and blames Pat for not calling him to be there earlier.
2. John gathers others thirty minutes early and covers things Pat needs to know, and then blames her for being late.
3. John arrives at the meeting on time, but keeps everyone waiting twenty minutes while he stays on the phone talking with his wife (or daughter, son, mother, doctor . . .). If Pat expresses her irritation at this waste of time, he gets on her case.

Remember ─────────────────────────────

The PA's primary goal is to provoke you in order to control you, and then to deny doing it.

True Life

True-Life Adventure 2:
Despicable Dan and Vicki

Dan assigns Vicki a large share of the work on a project that she completes. Dan, then schedules a meeting for himself with the higher-ups and takes sole credit for the work done. When Vicki later confronts Dan about this, Dan's comeback is that Vicki should be thankful that she is on the team in the first place and that she is getting good experience. He further tells her that she should be working for the good of the company, not for her own glory, and that is what should matter.

At first, Vicki considers Dan's comments but then realizes that, once again, she is being manipulated. When Vicki persists in her challenge, Dan gets personal. He tells Vicki, "I think you're being too selfish and self-centered, don't you think? Individual egos should be left at home. You're not appreciating all I'm doing for you."

Remember ―――――――――――――――――――――――――

PAs are masters at being elusive. It is crucial that you stay in contact with how the PA is making you feel. The main indicators that a PA is playing you are frustration, being put on the defensive, and anger. That is where the PA wants you: confused, angry, and guilty that you lost control. The PA will never address the issue at hand but will change the topic to you and your problems.

True Life

True-Life Adventure 3:
Blameless Becky and Trusting Karen

Becky is Karen's coworker on a project. She has Karen's special cell-phone number so she can call Karen about an important meeting over the weekend. Becky, however, calls one of Karen's other numbers. She never calls the number Karen specifically gave her until ten minutes before the meeting when Karen is fifty miles away.

"I don't know why you're upset with me. I *did* call you," Becky later says huffily to Karen. She then tells Karen about how much time and effort she put into calling her.

"But, Becky, why didn't you call the number I gave you?" Karen asks in frustration.

Becky replies, "I did my job and called you. It's not my fault you're so difficult to reach."

Remember ―――――――――――――――――――――――――

PAs undermine and take no responsibility. If there is any blame, it is yours.

True Life

True-Life Adventure 4:
Petty Pete and Meg

Meg's assistant Pete is a PA. Pete believes he deserves a lot more than he is getting in his job and life in general, and he shows his discontent by parking his car in Meg's place each day . . . by mistake. Pete is intentionally yanking Meg's chain, and when she complains to him, he tries to make her look petty.

Pete does not pull his weight in his job, procrastinates in getting things done, and frequently appears at the human resources department with some new grievance. When asked to do some task, Pete grumbles and moans and usually gripes that he is already overburdened. He has many complaints, but no solutions. When Pete is late with his part of a project, he blames others.

Being a true PA, Pete believes he is doing a better job than anyone else. If another person complains about him, Pete knows that others are jealous over his work and views it as another example of how others are out to make his life hard.

Pete is a backstabber. He will lie to you so convincingly that you will come away wondering if you had your facts straight. He taunts, provokes, and gives "constructive" criticism, but he can never take criticism in return. A typical conversation in the office might go as follows:

"Pete, we're meeting in five minutes. Where's that information you were supposed to have for me yesterday?" Meg asks.

"I didn't think you really wanted that information," Pete replies. "Besides, you gave me so much other work, how did you expect me to do it all? I'm only human, not a machine. Don't you understand that?"

Remember —————————————————————————————

PAs obstruct any positive team effort. They demoralize rather than help.

Picture This

Personal Life

The PA's need to control with guilt is especially dangerous in personal relationships. PAs take advantage of your sense of trust and fairness. They exploit your assumption that people who care for each other have the other's best interest in mind. PAs prey on your trying to be fair and reasonable. Personal relationships with PAs are always stormy, with interactions going from one argument to the next. PAs may appear to be appeasing, but it is only to set you up for another upset. Those prone to feeling guilty easily are most susceptible to the ways of PAs.

True Life

True-Life Adventure 1:
Spiteful Fred and Fiona

Fiona thinks she loves Fred, even though the guy drives her crazy. He is constantly doing things that get at her. Fred lives at Fiona's apartment because, as Fred tells it, the "bastards" at his old apartment would not work with him on his three-months' back rent. Fred did get even with them when he left by stuffing the toilets to overflow with waste and leaving garbage all around.

Fred does little to help around Fiona's place. He only does something when Fiona asks him, and even then he does a half-baked job in a sullen and dour way. One time, when Fiona complained about Fred's lackluster help, he "forgot" to leave the dog out for the millionth time, so Fiona had to clean up the mess when she came home from work. The rug was ruined. Fiona was angry and irritated not only at the mess, but also because she had to confront Fred, again, as to why this kept happening. Fiona erupted, "I feel like I'm talking to a child when I ask you to do things and help out. You get to brooding and take it out on me by 'forgetting' to do something, and then there's double work for me. You're like a resentful child who has to get even."

Fred showed no remorse or concern, nor did he give an apology. Filled with righteousness, he said, "I will not be treated like a child. How can I have an adult conversation with a screaming nag who's irrational? I keep hearing this over and over again. Can't you let it go?" As she always seems to do, Fiona started to feel bad for losing it and being unreasonable.

Remember

PAs trap you into thinking your behavior is wrong, and then exploit your perception.

True Life

True-Life Adventure 2:
Tom the Tormentor and Sally

Meet Tom, who is dating Sally. Tom is *always* late. He says to Sally, "If I call you to tell you I'll be late, you'll only get upset, so why should I call and have to take that crap?" On occasion, Tom forgets to pick up Sally entirely, but somehow it is Sally's fault. "You expect me to be perfect," he screams at her. Tom will invite Sally out, "forget" his money, and stick Sally with the check. He has no problem saying to Sally, "You make more money than I do, so why not spend it once in awhile?" If Sally says something about this, instead of apologizing, Tom goes on the attack and says, "I guess you have never forgotten anything, little Miss Perfect."

After much complaining, Tom agrees to go to a family get-together at Sally's brother's house. He is late getting ready, stops to get some beer to drink on the way, and, once there, gets drunk. When Sally confronts his behavior, Tom shows not a shred of insight into his childishness and lays the guilt back on her. "You *made* me come, so whatever I do is on your head, not mine," he says.

Remember

PAs want you to believe that you are controlling, dominating, and intrusive—not them. PAs rule with guilt.

True Life

True-Life Adventure 3:
Malicious Mike and Jane

Jane is in the hospital recovering from a serious operation. Her husband Mike calls her daily, not to see how she is doing, but to complain that he has no fresh laundry. As she lies in her hospital bed and listens on the phone, Mike criticizes her for not getting better sooner and coming home. "The doctors are keeping you there just to make more money off you, and you're milking it for all it's worth," he tells her. Mike does not bring the kids in to visit because it is "too much trouble," and "forgets" to bring Jane some clothes when it is time to go home. Mike gripes, "With the prices this place charges, it should supply a 'discharge outfit.'"

Once Jane is home to recuperate, Mike bellyaches all the more about his having no clean clothes and having to shop for food. When the kids act up, Mike tells Jane, "You should do something about *your* kids! And clean the house up— it's a pigsty. I don't know why I put up with this!" Jane thinks, *Am I supposed to be feeling guilty for getting ill and causing Mike all of this inconvenience?*

While Jane was in the hospital, Mike was not only having an affair but brought the woman home to have sex in their bedroom. He left a used condom on the bedside table. When Jane found it, she hit the roof. When she confronted Mike with the evidence, he said, "*You* left it there. What's the matter, your memory going as well as your sex appeal, you fat cow?"

A few weeks later, Jane is now back to work, as well as caring for the house and kids, cooking, and doing the laundry. She is in a business meeting when Mike calls and interrupts her. He has left his glasses in her car. He does not volunteer to come over and get them, or even to meet Jane halfway. He guiltifies Jane into bringing the glasses to where he is, and then, instead of a thank-you, Mike says, "God, you're really dumb to bring these over." He makes sure he says this in front of someone else.

Remember

PAs are resentful, abrasive, and unaccommodating people who will never be happy, despite anything you might do. PAs need their negativity to keep you at a distance. The only thing you share with a PA is misery.

True Life

True-Life Adventure 4:
Offensive Orin and Beth

After two years, Orin finally got around to changing the locks on the house while Beth is away on a trip. He's at work when Beth comes home and finds she cannot get into the house. When he finally arrives home, Orin says, "This is the thanks I get for interrupting my afternoon football and doing something for you!"

Remember ——————————————————————————

PAs have not a clue about how they irritate others, and they do not care.

True Life

True-Life Adventure 5:
Boorish Brenda and Curt

Brenda, the ex-wife, has the kids for the weekend. She calls her ex-husband, Curt, at his place and leaves a message changing the drop-off place *after* he has left his apartment to pick up the kids. Curt waits for an hour at the original drop-off spot and becomes more alarmed that something has happened to his kids. Another trick Brenda frequently pulls is not telling Curt how long she will be keeping the children. When he phones, Brenda will not talk to him. She puts one of the kids on the phone and says, "Tell Dad you want to stay here longer. If he doesn't like it, ask him why he is being so mean and not letting you stay and have fun with Mom."

Remember ——————————————————————————

PAs provoke and provoke some more. They do not change. You will always be frustrated if you believe that you can deal with PAs in a fair and reasonable manner.

DISCUSSION

PAs are very aggressive, but in an underhanded and indirect way; the "passive" part of *passive-aggressive* means that they are not directly confrontational. PAs are very negative and angry people who never deal with issues directly. They express their anger by their lack of cooperation. They are aggressive in their undermining, sabotaging, and instigating. They can also be sullen, pouty, and silent as they try to use this behavior to make other people feel guilty. They never discuss things, and they never say they are sorry—because whatever has happened is always someone else's fault anyway. Given that they cannot share, PAs cannot have close and intimate relationships. Their behavior style is focused on keeping other people under control, which prevents any closeness or intimacy.

The DSM-IV (*The Diagnostic and Statistical Manual of Mental Disorders,* Fourth Edition) describes PAs as showing a pervasive pattern of negativistic attitudes and passive resistance to demands for adequate performance. PAs usually have several of the following behaviors:

- Passively resisting the fulfilling of routine social and occupational tasks through procrastination and inefficiency.
- Complaining about being misunderstood and unappreciated.
- Acting sullen and argumentative in response to expectations.
- Scorning and criticizing authority.
- Envying and resenting people who are apparently more fortunate, which is everyone.
- Exaggerating one's own personal misfortune, while whining and grumbling.
- Alternating between hostile defiance and avoidance.

PAs are mostly males, although data show that women are slowly making inroads into this type of behavior. PAs were the defiant and oppositional kids you knew growing up, the "you can't make me" type. As adults, they do not change much. If you feel as if you are dealing with a two-year-old, you may be dealing with a passive-aggressive personality. When confronted, they are the ones who dig in their heels and are stubborn and obstinate. PAs will:

- Do or say something nasty to provoke you.
- Get you to respond in a fairly predictable way (you will be irritated, angry, defensive, confused, apologetic).
- Provoke you some more.
- Turn your response against you.

Remember

As with all personality disorders, first and foremost be aware of how the PA makes you feel. Use this awareness and knowledge to deal with the PDI rather than being used and manipulated. People with personality disorders use your feelings to control you. PAs elicit feelings of guilt.

The Contrasts That Confuse You
How People with Passive-Aggressive People Personality Disorder . . .

See Themselves	Want to Be Perceived
Long-suffering	Unappreciated
Discontented	Justified
Misunderstood	The poor little boy or girl
Justifiably resentful	Envious (of the more fortunate)
Luckless	Ill-starred
Jinxed	Hard-working
Victimized	Forlorn
Righteous	Deserving
Responsible	Supportive
Unrewarded	Independent
Self-made	Free
Autonomous	Self-determined

How PAs Will Appear to You if They Trap You

Wary	Ill-treated
Hurt by others	Susceptible
Sensitive	Disappointed
Vulnerable	Controlling
Needy	Unfortunate
Unappreciated	Needing someone to love them

How PAs Will Appear to You if They Trap You *(cont'd)*

Misunderstood	Challenging
Unloved	Strong-willed
Victimized	Lonely
Let down by life	Ill-starred
Deserving	Languishing

How PAs Should Appear to You if You Are *Not* Trapped by Them

Controlling	Unreasonable
Faultfinding	Indignant
Manipulative	Rationalized
Critical	In denial
Guiltifying	Obstructionistic
Sour/complaining	Sabotaging
Provocative	Undermining
Undermining	Oppositional
Procrastinating	Defiant
Quarrelsome	Contrary
Morose	Negative
Sullen	Resentful
Rude/insulting	Abrasive
Argumentative	Immature
Contemptuous	Irresponsible

Remember ————————————————————————

  How are they making you feel?

————————————————————————————————————

A TYPICAL CONVERSATION WITH A PA: NICK THE PAIN IN THE NECK AND PAT

Pat has been waiting for Nick to pick her up from work.

Pat: "I've been waiting for you for an hour in the rain. What happened?"

Nick: "Do you know what a pain it is to have to pick you up? The traffic this time of day? The time I've wasted? For your information, I was staying later at work to make more money for you to spend."

Pat: "Why couldn't you simply come on time? The kids are hungry. I have to do some food shopping."

Nick: "Screw the kids! They'll be okay. You pamper them too much as it is. You know what? You're spoiled . . . like I'm your slave or something. Can't you say, 'Thanks for picking me up' instead of bitchin'?"

How do you feel reading this? Most people feel angry with this insensitive idiot, yet many people, especially women, might feel guilty that they upset him. However, whether you feel angry or guilty, you are trapped.

From this point in the conversation, you can either be ensnared or not, depending on how you respond. Remember that they will drive you crazy—if you let them!

Typical Angry Response to the PA

Pat: "You selfish bastard! Just thinking how inconvenient it is for you. You can stick this ride . . ." Then there is silence and you are upset with yourself for letting him get to you, for losing control, and then for the eventual guilt and your apology.

Typical Guilty Response to the PA

Pat: "I'm sorry, you're right. You took the time, had a hard day, and I'm only adding to it." While you are saying this, you are confused as to why you are saying it and upset with yourself for doing so.

How You Will Feel in Dealing with the PAs

Confused	"*What* is he talking about?"
Angry	"He did it, and *I'm* to blame?"
Defensive	"Let me explain, it's not like you say."
Guilty	"Maybe I am to blame. I did get pretty angry."
Perplexed	"Wait a minute, what's going on here?"
Used/manipulated	"Somehow, I've just been suckered."
Controlled	"I couldn't get out of the corner I was in."
Victimized	"He did it, and *I* feel bad."
Frustrated	"I couldn't get my point across at all."
Trying to understand	"It's not him, it's all the stress he's under."
Foolish	"Was I dumb to fall for that."

How You Will Feel in Dealing with the PAs *(cont'd)*

Avoidant   "Why talk to him? It goes nowhere."
Inadequate   "If only *I* could explain things better and get him
                            to understand."

What one woman told me describes it well: "I was upset . . . angry . . .
yelling. So I felt more guilty. In all of the time in our relationship, he forever made me feel like it was my fault even though I *knew* it wasn't."

How to Deal with PAs

What You Cannot Do

- Expect them to change.
- Get provoked and allow yourself to get angry (overreact, argue, challenge, rant, get emotional in any way).
- Lose control.
- Feel guilty.
- Defend yourself and try to explain.
- Expect a reasonable discussion.
- Expect them to take on any responsibility or blame.
- Keep being dumb (if it does not work, do not keep doing it!).
- Rely on them to do what they say.
- Keep on discussing (that is, let them go on about *your* problem and what you should do).
- Question why they do what they do (after all, it is *your* fault).
- Try to get them to understand your side.
- Try to understand their point of view ("If only I could understand him/her, this wouldn't happen").
- Avoid them because of how you are feeling and expect them to reconsider.
- Keep being surprised when they do not change.
- Get off the issue.
- Accept the excuses.
- Tell them what to do.
- Threaten.
- Enable (let it happen repeatedly).

Remember

If it doesn't work, don't keep doing it!

How to Deal with the PAs
What You Can Do
(Do these mainly to keep your perspective.)

- Expect *no* change.
- Be firm and observe (like you are watching a movie).
- Remind yourself that you are being provoked, and stay objective.
- Define how *you* see the situation (especially to yourself).
- Have facts to undermine their denial.
- Present how things are (do a reality check).
- Assert yourself.
- Be silent (do not get sucked into an argument).
- Repeat their words back to them.
- Keep to the point.
- Suggest alternatives and make it clear that they have the choice about what they can do.
- Confront their behavior.
- Use their behavior against them.
- Play innocent: "I'm only giving my opinion . . . you're free to do whatever."
- Explain you are proud of whatever you are being attacked for: "Yes, I am speaking out, and it's what I need to do for myself instead of being a wuss."
- Play the failure: "I have to admit that I am an awful person and not who you want me to be. Thank you for constantly reminding me of my flaws. You're a saint to put up with me. How do you do it?"
- Firmly tell them what you are going to do and make it not dependent on them.

Remember

If you do the above, expect the PA to get worse.

With confrontation, a PDI will worsen, *especially* if the person is a PA. You are confronting not in hopes of changing him or her, but to save your sanity and not let the situation go on forever, which it will if you let it.

TYPICAL CONVERSATION: REVISED
(AFTER PAT READ THIS CHAPTER)

Pat: "I've been waiting here in the rain for an hour. What happened?"
Nick: "Do you know what a pain it is to pick you up? The traffic? The

time it takes me? For your information, I was staying at work to make more money for you to spend."

Pat: "I admit that I was dumb relying on you since you're almost always late."

Nick: "I'm the dumb one for doing things for you, coming to get you, listening to your complaining. That's gratitude for you. Not even a thank-you for my being here."

Pat: "That's okay. I won't bother you in the future. I'll find another way to get home."

The exception to the above is dealing with a boss or other higher-up since you do not want them angry with you. Unless you are very manipulative yourself (and this probably means you have your own problems), the best thing to do if you have an individual like this is to transfer to another department or leave. Whether you use reason, fairness, common sense, or guile, you are not likely going to win this one. The amount of mental energy you will put into "winning" is not worth it, and you are not in a position to confront.

THE TYPES OF PEOPLE WHO ARE MOST TRAPPED IN RELATIONSHIPS WITH PAS

PAs have snagged us all. However, since these people are so negative to be around, most of us avoid them. If you are bound into a relationship with a PA, look at your vulnerabilities.

If you are a caring person, you might be staying in the relationship with the notion that you will work things out. You are bewildered and challenged by the PA's behavior, but you are resolved to make the relationship right. You may have taken the blame initially, erring on the side of trying to be overly fair. *PAs do not change.* If you continue to allow yourself to be used and abused, you must look at your own issues. Since PAs play on guilt, they frequently exploit those with problems, insecurity, or guilt, or those who have been abused previously.

Remember ———————————————————————

You think that being a good and helpful person will help PAs. You will not save them. You will never *make them happy. You will only be miserable.* Remember: *If it doesn't work,* don't keep doing it!

SUMMARY

PAs are sullen, negative individuals who control you with guilt. They complain, whine, and exaggerate their own misfortunes at the hands of others, yet they are usually the ones who provoke their own undoings. They complain about being misunderstood, which is often another way to trap you.

CHAPTER 3

The Dramatic, Emotional, and Erratic, Who Overwhelm and Control You with the Power of Their Personality: The Histrionic Personality Disorder (HPD)

The Seductress . . . Emotional, Attention-seeking, Needy, and Always Putting on a Show

"Do you like my outfit? Oh my God, I'm going to die. You're so wonderful, and to think we've only just met."

Key Point: Histrionic personality disordered (HPD) individuals exude behavior filled with drama, superficiality, and emotion. These people (more often women than men) are the true drama queens. HPDs are emotionally unrestrained and use a strong emotional style to attract your attention. They do this by being personable, flirtatious, coy, lively, and seductive, or they embellish physical and/or emotional problems to gain your concern or attention. Because of their insatiable need for attention, HPDs use whatever is at their disposal to catch your eye. They are charmers who use their personalities, their looks, their dress, and their behaviors to attract you. HPDs are people of extremes. Everything is the best, the worst, or the most . . . or never, always, or forever. Nothing is in between.

The insecurity of HPDs is so profound that they must always have you around noticing them; thus, they confirm that they have worth. For HPDs, even negative attention is better than no attention at all. Once the HPD ensnares you with her appeal, you will be presented with her neediness, which she further uses to trap you into a relationship. The HPD is not interested in you as a person but rather in what you represent to her in terms of strength, power, and security. To the HPD, all relationships are superficial.

In her search for a powerful and stable figure on whom she can rely (invariably a man), the HPD frequently conjures up the role of the needy heroine seeking rescue by the white knight, her hero. Men are most often trapped into the HPD's web in this fashion. Most men love to be heroes.

If you are a woman witnessing the antics of an HPD, very likely your reaction of resentment and indignation at the HPD's superficiality and brash, attention-seeking behavior will control you. However, you may initially be taken in by the HPD's playing of the poor, downtrodden role. The HPD will manipulate you by using your anger against you as she portrays you as one more heartless person attacking a poor innocent.

Because of their intense need for praise and attention, HPDs need to be around people. Therefore, you will frequently encounter them in daily life. They know how to work the crowd in shamelessly attracting the attention, concern, help, and sympathy of others. HPDs convey a commanding physical or dramatic presence. Once they know they have your attention, HPDs very quickly give evidence of their suffering and hardship.

Red-Flag Feelings in You

Strong sexual or emotional appeal
Desire to rescue
Anger

Picture This

Who Are the HPDs You Might See?

You are at a party. An attractive woman enters the room and is speaking more loudly than anyone else. All eyes turn to her in her low-cut dress and abundance of jewelry. As she goes from one person to another (some she does not know) and embraces them like long-lost friends, she emotes, "Don't let me interrupt, please ignore me [as her voice becomes louder and more intense]. I'm sorry for being so late. The driving was the most treacherous I've ever experienced in my life. I was close to death at least three times! I'm a shattered wreck! I'll never drive again! My doctor warned me that I would die *immediately* if I had any alcohol, but I desperately need something to calm this shattered psyche. Look how I'm shaking and how cold my hands are," as she grasps the hands of the nearest male. Several people hasten to her to hear the full story and comfort her in her distraught state. They never quite get the details as to how she was close to death. The hostess stares and is perplexed as to how someone on one hand can look so perfect (in makeup, hair, dress, etc.), can smile and be so enchanting, and yet claim to be so distressed at the same time. She suspects events have been a little overembellished. The solicitous host ensnared by the drama of his guest's suffering runs to her aid. While he is being supportive, he also checks out her cleavage.

Remember

The HPD is dramatic, superficial, and attention-seeking.

A mother tells her sixteen-year-old child, "I must face the fact that you will be leaving me someday and utterly break my heart. If I seem more distant to you, it is because I want to prepare for that awful heartbreak since you are the only thing that brings me happiness in my miserable life with your vicious and uncaring father."

Remember

The HPD is self-centered and manipulative.

Think of the aging sixty-year-old in spandex trying to be twenty-five who laments, "I am getting old. No one wants you when you're old." Or the shapely twenty-five-year-old in spandex who complains, "All those men are always staring at me. Why do they do it? A girl can't dress the way she wants without someone ogling her. Do they really think I want the attention?"

Or think of Marilyn Monroe, a bright, beautiful, and famous woman seeking a "strong" man in her life (Joe DiMaggio, the ball player, for physical strength; Arthur Miller, the playwright, for intellectual power). As the memorable four-story-tall picture of her with her dress being blown up was unfurled in Times Square to advertise *The Seven-Year Itch,* she is said to have remarked, "This is the only way they think of me." She sure did get the attention.

Remember

HPDs are coy and suggestive. They watch others watch them.

Picture This

Professional Life

By virtue of your expertise in your role as the professional, the consultant, or the expert in your field, the HPD automatically portrays you as a person of strength and power. Although she will seek out your help for anything from vague and intangible to very specific reasons, the HPD loses that focus to her primary need of engaging your interest.

HPDs are extremely adaptive in attempts to maintain your attention. If an HPD thinks your attention is worth having, she will expand upon her problems or needs related to your area, challenge you more to help her, and appeal to your ego. When you think you have solved one problem, she will bring in more.

Remember

The HPD's problems are only vehicles to get and keep your interest in her.

You might hear these statements from a histrionic person:

"I'm so upset, I can't talk about it" (as she proceeds to tell you *all* about it). "I could tell I could immediately trust you as soon as you entered the room. I've seen a *million* specialists, but you're the *first* I feel comfortable with."

"I just *know* you are the very best person to help me."

"It's tremendously urgent that I speak *only* with you immediately. Otherwise, I don't know what I may do" (for a problem that has been present for four years).

"I have repressed my whole life from infancy. Devil worshipers sexually tortured me then. I just know it. No, I have no proof. . . . I just know it and only you can help with my tormented past."

"You're the *first* person I have ever told my deepest secrets to."

"I don't know how these problems occurred, but I know I can now feel safe with you helping me."

Consider the sixty-year-old woman seeking help from a psychiatrist. She is wearing her sunglasses as she enters his office in a slow, dramatic way. Warily, she looks around the office before sitting down. She says to the doctor, "I have a mental disorder. I have had years of fruitless treatment, but I cannot tell you what's wrong with me. My last psychiatrist told me he doesn't want to treat me anymore. That crushed me, but I didn't like him anyway."

She described her marriage as one where she was "a child of abuse who grew up into a wife of abuse. I would leave him, but I cannot be alone. I am suicidal every day, but I would never do anything."

Despite being plain and moderately obese, she noted to the doctor, "I have had many troubles with doctors who could not keep their hands off me."

Remember

The HPD will be vague, helpless, innocent, long-suffering, and prone to exaggeration. You will not easily get specifics from her.

A new client meets a financial advisor. She wants his advice on how she can invest her money to save to have a face-lift. She explains, "I am thirty-five, and my son is four. I want him always to remember me as young, not old and wrinkled. That's the reason I'll have the surgery, and I'll do it over and over. It's for him. I'm protecting him from disappointment. Please help me." Taken in by this unique request, the investment guy hunkers down to see how he can help this sensitive and unselfish woman.

Remember ———————————————————————

The HPD appears to be sensitive and responsive to others when she is actually self-serving and shallow.

———————————————————————————————

The characteristics of an HPD who comes to a professional for counseling or treatment are often as follows:

- Demanding immediate attention from everyone in your office from the moment (or even before) she arrives.
- Always dealing with some extreme in her life: things are either abysmal or wonderful.
- Speaking in fuzzy generalities and impressions, rarely giving facts.
- Frequently overwhelming with perfume, and often dressed well if not seductively.
- Reminding you that, although she looks fabulous, she is really "smiling through her suffering."
- Rarely following your advice or counsel.

The HPD has come to you, the professional/her hero, for guidance, help, and delivery from the victimization she endures. Her problems are never simple, and even if they are, they are presented as being of a catastrophic nature. She believes that she is the victim and that you, the expert, will take it away and make it all better.

Since your role as the professional really is to give counsel, advice, direction, and help, this situation at first does not appear inappropriate. However, as your time with the HPD continues, you will find yourself in an increasingly frustrating and losing situation since she never actually heeds your advice. If you become angry with this, it makes her cry ("You don't understand. Why are you so demanding and mean? You know how sensitive I am"). If you patronize her, you will be perceived (rightly so) as callous and cold. If you keep trying to help and expect her to follow your counsel, you become frustrated at your increasing inadequacy and inability to get through (even though you always have been helpful to others in the past). The HPD may remind you of your failings to try and make you work harder.

Remember

Your role as a professional is to be there, nothing more.

The HPD will tell you about her suffering, her being a naïve and guileless person victimized by others, an uncaring and hurtful world, her being alone and not being able to trust anyone, her need for help and direction . . . until *you* came along: "Doctor, I can't endure the pain any longer. You are my *last* resort. I know *you* are the one who will bring me some peace from the torture I face every second of every day of my life." Curiously, her dress and appearance are not consistent with other patients you have seen for such serious problems. Her perfume may be just a little overpowering. She just came from shopping, she will be going out tonight to a dinner party, she is smiling and laughing; all this provides the context for her story of endless torture.

She'll throw you a challenging bone to chew on: "No one knows how much I've suffered and endured . . . from birth. I'm not sure I can talk about it. Please help me." Your client is entrancing, charming, attractive, alluring, suffering, dramatic, coy, and needy, but mainly she is in search of rescue. Her continuing extreme problems are her way of keeping your attention. The dramatic depths of her suffering pull you in to help her.

As the expert, you have the obligation and desire to help this person with her problems. However, when you are feeling compelled to save her from these insufferable problems in her life, to become her hero and to rescue her where so many others have failed (which she will tell you), then you are hooked and her control begins.

Remember

HPDs ensnare you with your desire to help by providing your service. They have problems, and you have answers. As long as they suffer and keep you interested, they have you.

Not infrequently and without prompting, and within a few minutes of meeting you, the HPD will speak of sexual matters, including her past and present flirtations, and her sex life, sex practices, fantasies, or frustrations. Alternatively, the HPD might discuss sex in a guileless innocence as she describes her disgust for men who are "only interested in one thing" and are always coming on to her. You will note that she may dress very provocatively or that she has a coy and playful manner. If you are a man and comment on this, you will fall into the "you're just like all the rest" category. If you are a woman who comments, the HPD will tag you as jealous of her femininity.

Remember

Seductiveness is one of the ways HPDs keep your attention. She may flatter you, bring you gifts, or change or escalate her problems if your interest wanes. She may also try to seduce you sexually. It depends on how much she thinks she needs you.

One New York model went to her new doctor looking plain and ordinary with no makeup and dull clothes. She told him, "I didn't want my looks to distract you. I really want your help." She nonetheless showed him her recent swimsuit photos.

A plastic surgeon performed a breast enlargement operation on a female patient. She inflated his ego as she praised his work. She dropped by the office with gifts for this talented man. She asked for and he scheduled frequent breast "exams." They found themselves often in his car as they met to look through copies of *Penthouse* magazine to compare his work. Fortunately, other medical colleagues got his attention and reminded him of his commitment to medical ethics before this farce progressed any further.

Remember

An HPD's only reason for giving attention to you is to prep you for giving her all of your attention in the future.

True Life

True-Life Adventure 1:
Mournful Mary and Dr. Bob

Dr. Bob, a psychiatrist, first met Mary when she consulted him for the "inhumane suffering" she was experiencing at the hands of her ex-husband and mother (Mary was forty-two). Mary was impeccably dressed. In her first appointment, she described her life experiences, each one more horrendous than the one before. Mary told Dr. Bob of her hateful and self-centered mother who called her daily to taunt her on what a failure she was. There were the men who used her for sex, her sixteen-year-old daughter who abused and scorned her, an ex-husband who had physically abused her (and still harassed her), the school system that terrorized her son, the lawsuit for sexual harassment against a former boss for trying to bed her, the crooked lawyers and judges who were bought off by her former employer, and her financial misery. There was the constant job changing since she could not tolerate the abuse from jealous female managers. Finally, she had turned forty and mourned that she had lost her attractiveness. Would the strong man she needed now spurn her?

"What man will look at me now with all of those young, blond Barbies out there? Dr. Bob, I don't know what to do. *Please* help me," she implored. Mary—who was not only physically attractive, but was also bright (Phi Beta Kappa), articulate, and a great storyteller—had Dr. Bob's attention. After hearing about her sad life, he was overwhelmed at how much this poor woman had endured. As Mary talked, Dr. Bob reviewed in his mind the many ways that he was sure he could help, including Mary's search for love and the errors she had unconsciously made with men in her quest for acceptance.

"By the way," Mary added, "you should also know that my father may have sexually molested me, although I still think of him as the only hero in my life." Dr. Bob knew Mary had come to the right place. This needy person had found the caring professional to help her.

Mary's experiences were real, and she indeed suffered from all of the above. But her suffering also brought her the attention she craved. To give up this lifestyle would mean she would lose this way of gaining attention, and that was not an option. Her stories of torment were always punctuated with the phrase, "It gets better," and the stories did!

Although Mary enthusiastically welcomed his interpretations of her behaviors and his suggestions on how to improve her life, Dr. Bob became frustrated by seeing Mary make few changes in her life, which continued to be filled with strife and dramatic situations. Mary's unrelenting pleas for help served only to make Dr. Bob double his resolve to save her. Poor Dr. Bob.

Remember

An HPD may have serious problems for which she legitimately seeks your professional help, but these issues are secondary to her need for your noticing her. The HPD cannot improve, because that would take away her means of getting the attention in the first place.

True Life

True-Life Adventure 2:
Downcast Denise and the Lawyer

Denise: "Thanks for seeing me without an appointment. I know you told me not to see my soon-to-be ex again (especially after you went to such extremes to get the restraining order), but I just had to see him one more time. He sounded so depressed. When you gave me your private number the last time I was in, I felt so special. I can't forgive myself for calling you at 2 am the other night when my husband started threatening me. I always feel so much more reassured when I talk with you."

Lawyer: "What did he threaten?"

Denise: "Oh, I don't remember specifically, but it wasn't nice. I felt like he was going to attack me or rape me."

Lawyer: "What did he do?"

Denise: "I don't want to talk about it, I can't remember. But I just felt he was going to do something. He was angry, you know, about my taking all of the furniture out of the house while he was at work and emptying all of the bank accounts and pouring paint remover over the hood of his vintage Corvette. He's such a child."

Lawyer: "Why did you see him again? I specifically advised you against doing that. You miss our appointments, come in unannounced with some grave problem, call me with 'emergencies,' yet you don't seem to follow any of my recommendations."

Denise: "I do listen to you. I try so hard to follow through with everything you say, but it's so hard. I know you like blue from the way your office is decorated. How do you like my dress? Can't we talk about this over a drink? It's so formal here in your office."

Lawyer: "That's really not the issue. Did he do something to hurt you?"

Denise: "No. Why would he hurt me?"

Lawyer: "You said he was threatening you."

Denise: "Oh, that. It really wasn't quite threatening. Please don't yell at me. My ex would do that. Please don't be like him. Do you care about me? Or am I just another client? I thought you were a person with some sensitivity and concern."

Lawyer: "I do have concerns about you. That's why I am puzzled why you ask my advice and never follow it."

Denise: "Please be patient with me and give me another chance. I'll be good."

Remember

Despite seeking you out as though you were the wisest person in the universe, the HPD does not trust you. She may make it seem as though you are in charge, but you are not.

True Life

True-Life Adventure 3:
Karen Comehither and Will, the Social Worker

Professionals, no matter how experienced they think they are, recurrently fall prey to HPDs' beguiling charms. HPDs are mistresses of flirtation, sexual magnetism, ego stroking, and seduction. If a professional is to commit the egregious mistake of having sexual relations with a client or patient, it will most likely be with an HPD.

Karen sought Will out for serious counseling regarding her alcohol use, her depression, and her loneliness. Karen told Will that she felt as worthless as a "ten-cent piece of dirty ice." In the first appointment, Karen volunteered information about her intense sex life, her sexual fantasies, and her desires. Will used all of his skill to remain professional, but he still had a tough time not imagining the sexual scenes Karen created. After a few appointments, Karen said, "I look forward all week to seeing you, Will. I feel so much better after we talk."

Karen would drop by at other times and leave little presents for Will to show her appreciation for his help. She would find reasons to linger with Will at the end of the appointment and requested to have the last appointment of the day when it was "quieter" (and when other personnel had left). Will's smart side told him to be careful, but his dumb side rationalized, "It's not hurting anything, and I don't want to seem cold and rejecting." At the end of one appointment, Karen asked for a hug "to feel reassured." The hug led to a kiss on the cheek, which led to a longer and lingering kiss, which led to sex. Will thought to himself, *I know some people would consider this unethical, but this is a special case. Karen needs someone she can trust, someone who can make her feel desirable again.*

Unfortunately, Karen kept drinking and began to call Will at home (of course, he gave her this number) in the middle of the night in very emotional states. More unfortunate still, Will's wife answered the phone. Will was a hero no longer.

Remember

There is no relationship other than the one the HPD needs—the relationship of fantasized security. Although the HPD may compliment you, appeal to your vanity, and make you feel special, you do not exist as a person for the HPD. Your only worth is in how secure you can make her feel . . . and you can never help the HPD get the security she fantasizes after.

True Life

True-Life Adventure 4:
Wretched Wanda and Dr. Bob

Wanda, a former airline stewardess and girl-about-town, has on several occasions consulted with Dr. Bob, a psychiatrist, and lamented her terrible plight in extricating herself from her vicious and evil third husband. Wanda, who had been dropped as a patient by numerous doctors because of her demands on them for cures, meets with Dr. Bob to ask his advice on how she can find a new doctor.

Wanda (holding her sides and grimacing): "It hurts so much when I breathe. I've had pancreatitis, you know. I'm allergic to my house. There must be mold in the air ducts. I can't breathe there. The whole house smells of urine. I have people coming over for my mother's seventy-fifth birthday Saturday night. What will I do?"

Before Dr. Bob can respond, Wanda says, "I can't take it any longer. If I don't lose my mind, I must be crazy! I'll have to walk around at the party with an oxygen mask on." Dr. Bob tries to reassure Wanda and offer her suggestions. But he knows that she will likely go on like this for a few more minutes, thank him for his time, and then leave.

Remember

The HPD will not change . . . *no matter how good you think you are at what you do.*

Picture This

Business Life

In a business environment, the HPD manipulates others using either her sexual charms or neediness to influence and control. Not infrequently, the HPD uses the persona of the innocent, waiflike person requiring direction. She will exploit sexual harassment issues, a physical debilitation, or threats of scandal, lawsuits, or fiscal mayhem to manipulate those around her.

She is the coworker who exudes enthusiasm at the start of a project as long as she can occupy the center of attention.

She has many enthusiastic ideas that lack substance and thought. The HPD believes she should get points solely based on her exuberance.

Her energy wanes if she has to work in the background. She pouts, feeling rejected and unappreciated.

When the head of a project is a male, the HPD is the individual who may try to manipulate him with smiles and a friendly manner. If the project head is a female, she may use smiles but more often uses backstabbing and hints that an envious and petty boss is mistreating her in some way.

Remember

The HPD exudes warmth and neediness to get what she wants. When challenged, she can be venomous.

True Life

True-Life Adventure 1:
Lousy Lynne and Straight-Arrow Sally, Her Manager

Lynne is always dressed well but with a hint of sexuality, in tight-fitting clothes, short skirts, or with the extra button of her blouse undone. Sally, her manager, always dresses in business attire with appropriate outfits. Sally is businesslike, organized, and goal-directed. She gets along with her staff because she treats them with respect, although Sally can also be firm when she has to be. Lynne gets on with her coworkers by schmoozing with the guys and enlisting sympathy from the women.

Sally: "Lynne, we have this report due, and I need that information you were going to research."

Lynne: "Getting that information gave me a headache like a molten spike was being placed in my head, and I couldn't continue with it. Can you get someone else to do it right now? Are those figures that important?"

Sally: "You seemed to be having a good time over coffee just a few minutes ago. Has your headache abruptly returned?"

Lynne: "I am entitled to my coffee break. Why do you resent my few minutes of enjoyment? I can't help if I get along well with people and am popular. I'll get Jim to get those figures for you. You know, a little praise goes a long way with people rather than your vicious criticism."

Lynne later tells others how plain, ordinary Sally is jealous of her. She tries to split the loyalties of her coworkers in order to gain sympathy.

Lynne sees herself as a big-idea visionary, therefore not someone who should have to do the day-to-day work. Lately, Lynne's flirtatiousness and seeming openness are beginning to wear thin with her coworkers (even the men). Lynne fails to see that her behavior is putting people off.

If her job is threatened, she may seduce, threaten, or, sobbing deeply, plead for sympathy as she tells about her wretched and traumatic life or how unfairly she has been treated in her job. If you manage her, she needs constant support, encouragement, and praise. You might become the strong person she says she needs in her life. Comforting, consoling, and advising her will be a daily task. An employee like Lynne does not take on responsibility and work independently. She desires to work with the team, but only insofar as she can be the center of attention. If she is more cunning, she will forsake you and move up the corporate ladder by enticing, cajoling, and flattering higher-ups to be her mentor.

Remember

HPDs, although appearing independent and self-reliant, are high-maintenance.

True Life

True-Life Adventure 2:
Tragic Tess and Principal Poorbody

For many years, Tess has worked in the city school system where she has channeled her theatricality into teaching English drama. Her colleagues long considered Tess as flaky, but they tolerated her as long as she stayed in the background. That worked for Tess because she thrived on the attention she received from her students, many of whom were smitten with their artsy teacher.

Budget cuts placed more responsibility and demands on Tess. She became increasingly distressed. With the strain, her tendency to the melodramatic began to surface beyond the classroom. Tess began having increasingly more arguments with her department head and asked to speak with the principal. Tess paced in the principal's waiting area, wringing her hands and moaning aloud with her internal suffering. When finally asked in, she slowly walked to her chair, the many bracelets and baubles on her arms clanging away. Her hair was messy and frequently entangled in her huge, dangling earrings. Her hands were shaking.

Principal Poorbody said, "Tess, I can't understand the reason for your trouble with Tom [the department head]. You both seemed to have worked well together all these years."

Clutching her chest, Tess responded, "Do you know what that self-absorbed, obnoxious, obese oaf demanded of me? To teach remedial English. I have always trusted you. You know that my incredible talents with the more gifted students would be wasted there. When I go into that torturer's office, I have to keep myself from vomiting because of the stench that oozes from that place. I hold my sides to keep from retching. You know, he was tearing apart a donut as we talked. It was so symbolic, since he was also tearing me apart. You know, I believe that his fat comes from his feeding on the entrails of his victims. And I'm not going to be one of them!"

The principal breathed a heavy sigh.

Remember ―――――――――――――――――――――――――――――――――――

The HPD wows you with the drama but has little substance in what she says.

Picture This

Personal Life

The HPD is the siren, the vamp, the seductress. She is every man's fantasy . . . turned nightmare. She is the sorceress who at first seems giving and submissive, but who quickly takes control and manipulates you. The HPD initially lures you with hints of fulfilling your sexual fantasies or your ego's needs through her attention to you. She will definitely ensnare you with her neediness and offer you fulfillment in being her rescuer. Whatever avenue of fantasy you care to follow, she will be controlling you.

True Life

True-Life Adventure 1:
Cruel-Hearted Carla and Pete

Carla is Pete's dream girl. She is beautiful and personable, and she gets along easily with everyone she meets. Carla seems to have that vibrant connection with life. Pete, more an analytical, brainy type, sees Carla as bringing some color to his life. He is the practical side of the relationship while Carla is the emotional.

Sure, Pete thinks, *she can be moody and pouty, but that's because she's been treated badly in the past* (mostly by other men before Pete). Pete understands. He may have to organize Carla to get through the day with the more practical things of living like balancing the checkbook, getting self-service gas, or cleaning the apartment, but her warm smiles and bubbly personality more than make up for that. Carla constantly fishes for compliments, reassurance, and gifts, which Pete gladly showers on her.

Pete says, "I know work's been hard for you lately and you've been having more muscle pain, so I was passing this store and stopped in to buy you something."

Carla responds, "Oh, Pete. What is it? You're so wonderful. I really don't deserve anything. What is it? A ring? A necklace? You know how much I liked that watch I saw the other day. Or is it that blouse I loved?"

Carla opens the package and finds the bracelet she had also been recently admiring. She says, "Oh, Pete. It's *gorgeous;* it's what I've *always* wanted. No one has ever given me something this nice. When I was a little girl, I always imagined someone like you would do this for me. Now my dream has come true." Carla kisses Pete on the cheek, smiles, and says, "Maybe I'll thank you more later." Then she stares off for several minutes, puts the bracelet aside, and starts talking about a new pain in her arm. Pete feels bad that his gift is not quite enough to make Carla happy. He thinks, *How can I help her? How can I make her more secure? I try to give it all to her, and it's still not enough. Why can't I give her some happiness? Why can't I measure up? If only her anguish were not so intense.*

Pete is confused and disappointed. Being the nice guy he is, he blames himself for the situation and fails to see that Carla can never be satisfied or happy.

Remember ——————————————————————————

You can never be the source of happiness for anyone else, especially an HPD who thrives on her neediness to get her attention. The HPD believes this attention will give her security. When it inevitably does not, you can fall from being perfect to being inadequate in less than thirty seconds.

True Life

True-Life Adventure 2:
Critical Colleen and Bud

Colleen and Bud are at a restaurant for dinner with neighborhood friends, Betty and Fred. Colleen says, "It's been such a long week. Betty, I don't know how you put up with it all . . . and with your three kids. I could never take the demands kids place on you, and they need so much attention. I can see you pay a price for it. I could surely use more support, but Bud just doesn't listen."

Bud appears to be listening now and says, "What do you mean? All I see is your being out shopping all day. You don't clean, you don't cook. I shop, cook the meals, and do the laundry. Where does your stress come in?"

Ignoring Bud, Colleen goes on, "Betty, I know Fred helps you out and he doesn't complain. Bud just doesn't seem to get it together. We never talk, and when we do, it's always about something I'm not doing. It's always criticism. Is Fred tired at night? Is he able to . . . perform? Bud and I haven't had sex in a long time, and I hate to say it in front of everyone, but Bud has never been too much of a hero in that department either."

Remember

HPDs often attack a man's sexuality (if you are a woman, she assails your femininity) as a way of inspiring guilt and avoiding her own responsibility. The HPD tries to put you on the defensive because of your inadequacy in not being everything for her.

True Life

True-Life Adventure 3:
Innocent Ann and Lance

Lance was an MIT graduate engineer with a high-paying job. He was very analytical. Lance could tune his car, do plumbing, put in electrical wiring, fly a plane, build a house on his own, and basically solve most practical problems, but he was somewhat inept socially. He met Ann at a party thrown by friends and became immediately smitten with her extroverted personality. Lance was shy and reserved, and always had to think before he acted, and Ann's zany and spontaneous style enchanted him. Ann, in turn, was attracted to Lance's brilliance and stability, both intellectually and financially. She saw him as well-structured and organized, qualities that she lacked. Lance was not much of a talker, but that was okay with Ann, who could easily fill that role. Lance would frequently say to his friends, "Opposites attract." They married, but this happy union of opposites was not to last.

Lance was not confrontational, so he often avoided the issues that began to affect the orderly, structured world of his to which Ann was initially drawn. After much sweating and rehearsing, Lance finally sat down to talk with Ann. Looking at the floor, Lance began, "We've talked a little about your spending beyond our limits, but you continue to overdraw the checking account. I make a good living, but you are spending way above our means. Are you subtracting the amounts for the checks you write as well as the ATM withdrawals?"

Ann immediately was in tears: "You know I've never been any good with figures. Why do I have to deal with the checkbook? It's not my spending, but your being so tightfisted with the money. If you made more money, this wouldn't happen. I shouldn't have to have restrictions on me, for *all* I do for you. All of my friends' husbands make more than you do. They don't have to watch every penny. I thought you were kind and gentle and caring, but all you are is a selfish miser who doesn't appreciate me! I shouldn't have married so quickly. *Everyone* told me you were too rigid for it to work, but I thought there was some humanity in you. You know I *settled* for you? That was the biggest mistake in my life."

Lance never was able to fully discuss the issue of Ann's overspending. Each time he tried to get back to the subject, she cried and screamed more loudly than before. He felt like her tormentor on one hand while also feeling powerless in solving the problem. Lance's orderly and logical life slowly unraveled.

Invariably, the HPD's victim initially sees himself as this incredibly fortunate guy who, by some miracle, has attracted this charming, attractive, divine creature with seemingly fantastic social skills. The HPD sees him as her protector in navigating the unpleasant aspects of living. The unsuspecting male sees himself as the white knight who will rescue, help, and support this poor yet giving woman, who often comes with the baggage of being treated badly by others through no fault of her own.

Remember

After the allure has grown thin, HPDs wear you down with guilt. You become either silent and solitary or frustrated and fuming.

DISCUSSION

HPDs are the life of the party. They are vivacious, animated, coy, and enticing. They are the consummate charmers, gushing with emotionality and drama, and exaggerating profusely. Yet they are also manipulative, shallow, and self-centered. They are preoccupied with physical attractiveness or personal complaints, and they thrive on and seek out appreciation by others.

The DSM-IV (*The Diagnostic and Statistical Manual of Mental Disorders,*

Fourth Edition) describes HPDs as having a pervasive pattern of excessive emotionality and attention seeking, beginning in early adulthood. An HPD will generally exhibit five (or more) of the following behaviors or characteristics:

• Is uncomfortable in situations where he or she is not the center of attention.
• Interaction with others is often characterized by inappropriate sexually seductive or provocative behavior.
• Displays rapidly shifting and shallow expression of emotions.
• Consistently uses physical appearance to draw attention to self.
• Has a style of speech that is excessively impressionistic and lacking in detail.
• Shows self-dramatization, theatricality, and exaggerated expression of emotion.
• Is suggestible—that is, appears easily influenced by others or circumstances.
• Considers relationships to be more intimate than they actually are.

Histrionic personality disorder is found more frequently in women than in men. The HPD is the little girl in a woman's body who, despite the outward show, is seeking a hero who will supply security, protection, strength, and unconditional love.

HPDs appear to be outgoing and to have a very easy manner with others. They mix in either sexually provocative behavior or less explicitly coy, demure, and suggestive actions to attract interest. They may also elicit interest on more intellectual grounds, depending on the other person, but they always rely on an undercurrent of sexuality. What eventually draws you to the HPD is her neediness. The more "mature" HPD gets your attention in subtle but effective ways as she appeals to your intellectual and caring side to help her. The less mature HPD is out of control. She will cause scenes or perform other excesses (drinking, drugs, sexual liaisons, lying, fighting, hints at suicide) both to gain center stage and to bait you to help her regain control (you to the rescue, again). HPDs are initially quite pleasant to be with, but the rapidly shifting, superficial emotions they exhibit eventually wear thin. Unlike people with some other personality disorders, HPDs apologize for their behavior, but the apology is without sincerity and meaning since the behavior remains unchanged.

Although appearing to desire advice from a caring person to provide help, direction, treatment, counseling, structure, or guidance in their lives, HPDs will not follow or cooperate. Their stated need is just a way to draw you in. If they actually took your advice, it might make them dependent on you, which they must avoid since they cannot trust people. Dependency means submission, and submission means vulnerability. In the HPD's own mind (whether it's really understood or not), if she becomes vulnerable, she risks losing control of the situation, which means possibly losing attention—her prime goal. To the HPD, your attention means she is worth something, so she can never give up controlling you to get that attention.

Although HPDs act as though they have deep, passionate, and intimate relationships (like telling the plumber about her recent surgery "down below"), they usually have very superficial interactions with others. They rarely have close same-sex friends because of the threat of another woman stealing the scene. HPDs consider themselves a man's woman. As with all people who have personality disorders, the HPD harbors profound insecurities. She deals with them by having an attentive fan club. If you have attention, you must be desirable.

If you are a guy and feel you are dealing with a charmer who conveys the impression that she is a little waif in need of rescue, you probably are dealing with an HPD. If you are a woman and you are repeatedly shocked, indignant, or repulsed by the obviously manipulative behavior (especially sexual) of another female, you are dealing with an HPD. They repeatedly try to get your sympathy for their intense life suffering.

The following types of behavior identify an HPD personality:

- Provoking (usually pleasantly) by doing or saying something, often sexual in nature, to become the center of attention.
- Getting you to respond in a fairly predictable way (if you're a male, through sexual interest, charming you out of your socks, looking to you as a knight to the rescue; if you're a female, through feigning indignation, jealousy, or inadequacy).
- Flattering, stroking your ego, and seducing you in one way or another.
- Controlling you by charm or by guilt ("I trusted you but you keep letting me down").

Remember ————————————————————————

As with all personality disorders, first and foremost be aware of how the HPD makes you feel. Rather than being used and manipulated, use this awareness and knowledge to deal with her. People with personality disorders use your feelings to control you. HPDs make you feel captivated and then controlled by guilt or inadequacy or obligation.

The Contrasts That Confuse You
How People with Histrionic Personality Disorder . . .

See Themselves	Want to Be Perceived
Entertaining	Alluring
Captivating	Exciting
Outgoing	Playful
Too giving	Too loving and too sensitive
Unfulfilled	Innocent
Too adoring	Blameless
Misunderstood	Rejected
Needing a hero to rescue her	Needing stability
Exploited	Used
Ogled	Unappreciated
Cursed to be alone	Powerless
Suffering lost soul	Unfulfilled
Let down by others	Ultrafeminine
Too emotional	Uninhibited
Too honest	Needing to please
Bad (when not center of attention)	Envied by other women
Needing someone to trust	Discontented
Unable to trust	Passionate

How HPDs Will Appear to You If They Trap You

Independent	Adoring
Life of the party	Demure
Free-spirited	Misunderstood
Quickly intimate	Needing rescue
Seductive	Passionate
Mysterious	Socially at ease

How HPDs Will Appear to You If They Trap You *(cont'd)*

Alluring	Extroverted
Entrancing	A charmer
Coy	Witty
Teasing	A commanding presence
Playful	Suffering
Self-assured	Betrayed by others
Captivating	Hurt by life
Enticing	Naïve
Challenging	Trusting
Appreciative	Hero-maker
Experienced	A maiden in distress
Sensitive	Entertaining
Respectful	Appealing

How HPDs Should Appear to You If You Are *Not* Trapped by Them

Exhibitionistic	Overreactive
Self-absorbed	Overly sensitive
Dependent	Erratic
Needy	Theatrical
Vague	Attention-seeking
Superficial	Scornful of other women
Shallow	Impulsive
Confrontational	Frigid
Controlling	Lacking intimacy
Manipulative	Faultfinding
Guilt-inspiring	Forever victimized
Needing constant reassurance	A caricature of femininity
Never listening	Insecure
Unreliable	Capricious
Emasculating	Deceitful
Clingy	

Remember ──────────────────────────

How do they make you feel?

A TYPICAL CONVERSATION WITH AN HPD: CASTRATING KAREN AND REJECTED ROCCO

Rocco is sitting in the living room just staring at nothing when Karen seats herself on the sofa and draws her legs up beneath her. She takes time to arrange her dress and leaves a splash of thigh visible. She begins to cry softly but loud enough for Rocco to hear. Her brow is furled and her eyes downcast. She is making a circle with her finger on her left breast by the nipple. Despite the sound of crying, Rocco is perplexed because he sees no tears, and Karen is taking care not to ruin her eye makeup.

Rocco moves over next to her and puts his arm around her. He asks, "What's bothering you?"

Moving slightly away from Rocco, Karen continues to whimper for a minute or two longer, then lowers her hand from her breast and raises her eyes. She looks sorrowfully at him and says, "You're so cruel to me. You always blame me. I try so hard to please you and do what I think you want. I wore that sexy dress to the party tonight because I thought you like me to look good in front of your friends. Could I help it if one of them propositioned me? You embarrassed me so badly, I'll never be able to face any of them again. If I need to go out, I'll do it at night or go to another town just so I won't have to face any of them. This is the most awful thing that has ever happened to me in my life. I don't know how much more I can take. I wish I were dead. Where are my pills? What you did has brought back my pain all over again."

Rocco tries to be gentle in responding, "I don't know what to say. Please don't feel so bad. I admit that I got a little upset. You were, I thought, so flirty with the men, dancing in a very provocative way and not spending too much time with me. I guess I got jealous. Maybe I'm too possessive. You were just being sociable. I know you need your freedom."

Karen replies, "I thought you were attracted to me because of my outgoing personality. Now you condemn me for it. I don't know why you go to parties. You're always just standing around, not talking with anyone, just watching everyone else. When you do talk, it's so stilted, like you've never been around people before. At least I was able to get out and talk and laugh. At least *someone* noticed me! Why can't you be more human, have some feelings, and not be like a robot? You could have asked me to dance or gotten me a drink. You could have pushed your way in and got my attention. God knows, I've tried to bring out the man in you. Your friends are lots of fun. Not like you. What's wrong with a little flirting? Especially when your husband doesn't appreciate you. I was just having a little fun, but like all guys, you turn it immediately into something dirty and sexual. I try to give, to be open and friendly, but I'm always the used one to be thrown away and abused. Maybe if you gave me more attention, I wouldn't have to get noticed elsewhere."

Remember ───────────────────────────────

How do they make you feel?

───────────────────────────────

Typical Angry Response to the HPD

Rocco erupts: "Dammit! You married me because I was the strong, silent type, and now all you do is complain that I don't talk, feel, or communicate like you want. The house is a mess. God knows what you do around here. You don't cook. You don't clean. All you want to do is have a good time.

"You were coming on to every guy in the room before you had your coat off. You were hanging out of the dress and loved the attention. Yeah, it really ticks me off when you do that, and then when one of the guys starts to grab, I lose it. I should have fooled around with one of your friends. Oh, wait a minute, you don't have any women friends. They're all 'jealous' of you. It's not the first time. Why do you do it? You're a real piece of work. I'm going to bed. Which brings me to another thing: how you can be so hot at the party and so frigid in the sack?"

Typical Guilty Response to the HPD

In a subdued way, Rocco says, "I'm sorry. I know you've had a rough life, and I just seem to bring you down. I guess I get jealous of the other men and how you are with them. You're so beautiful and wonderful, I feel threatened that you'll find one of them more exciting and leave me. I'm sorry. I don't deserve you."

Typical Passive Response to the HPD

Rocco engages in silent submission as Karen continues to dramatize the situation.

How You Will Feel in Dealing with HPDs

At first . . .

If You Are Male

Charmed/dazzled/enchanted	"What a woman!"
Flattered	"I didn't know I was that good!"
Like a champion	"This poor woman needs my help."
Special	"She's interested in *me*."
Aroused	"What a babe."
Wrapped around her little finger	"She's so wonderful/She's suffered so."

If You Are Female

Motherly	"The *poor* thing."
Indignant	"What a hypocrite."
Angry	"She really plays people with that act. She's got them all fooled."
Frustrated	"She puts on like she doesn't know what's she's doing."
Jealous	"I have to admit, she does play it well."
Perplexed	"Is this person for real?"

Later . . .

For Males (Females Have Already Caught On)

Confused	"I thought I was the one."
Inadequate	"I just don't measure up to what she needs."
Guilty	"I can't make her happy."
Manipulated	"There goes that suicide threat again."
Angry	"You want my help but never follow it"; "You embarrass me in public"; "It's hard to deal with the drama all of the time."
Betrayed	"I give her all she wants and she still throws it up in my face."
Castrated	"She's got me."

One man described his frustration and anger in dealing with his HPD wife by saying: "She wants attention, I give her attention, or so I think. She wants help, money, security, I give it all, and it's still not enough. She continues to find fault with me in how I don't measure up, and she discusses it with anyone who'll listen."

Remember ──

You will never *be able to give her the attention she craves.*

───

How to Deal with HPDs
What You Cannot Do
- Be seduced and controlled by ego-stroking (intellectual seduction).
- Be seduced and controlled sexually.
- Feel too sympathetic.
- Expect to rescue her.
- Hope to make her happy.
- Hope to satisfy her.
- Expect to have a reasonable discussion.
- Expect her to change.
- Get angry (including silent fuming).
- Reassure in a grand manner ("Everything will be all better").
- Take responsibility for her life ("I'll make it all better").
- Believe events described are as severe as they are portrayed.
- Believe that she is as helpless as she seems.
- Believe that she will follow your advice.
- Trust her loyalty.
- Trust her at all.
- Question why.
- Get defensive.
- Get even by doing the same thing (having an affair, drinking, causing a scene).
- Be submissive to verbal and/or physical abuse.
- Patronize.
- Believe you are inadequate because she says so.
- Make fun of her.
- Be guilty.
- Stay feeling powerless.
- Believe she wants you.
- Expect her to be responsible.

Remember ————————————————————————

If it doesn't work, don't keep doing it!

————————————————————————

How to Deal with HPDs
What You Can Do
(Do these mainly to keep your perspective.)

- Remind yourself that she is always trying to seduce you in one form or another.
- Show reasonable concern and try to listen (no more than fifteen minutes).
- Acknowledge that she may have issues.
- Try to define issues.
- Accept being confused as a normal part of this relationship.
- Reassure reasonably ("I believe you'll get through this").
- Offer help/advice (knowing it will not be followed).
- Remind her that she does not have to go to extremes to get your attention.
- State that unacceptable behavior is unacceptable (be prepared as to what you are going to do about it).
- Assert what you feel a relationship should be like.
- Stay objective.
- Give examples of her problem behaviors without discussion.
- Be prepared for no change.
- Stand your ground.

Remember ————————————————————————

If you do the above, expect her to get worse.

————————————————————————

TYPICAL CONVERSATION: REVISED
(AFTER ROCCO READ THIS CHAPTER)

Rocco is sitting in the living room just staring at nothing when Karen seats herself on the sofa and draws her legs up beneath her. She takes time to arrange her dress and leaves a splash of thigh visible. She begins to cry softly but loud enough for Rocco to hear. Her brow is furled and her eyes downcast. She is making a circle with her finger on her left breast by the nipple. Despite the sound of crying, Rocco is perplexed because he sees no tears, and Karen is taking care not to ruin her eye makeup.

Rocco recognizes that Karen is trying to play on his sympathy about what happened earlier in the evening. He smiles inwardly and thinks, *Just like a soap opera.* Rocco pages through a magazine. He is silently waiting as he knows Karen will somehow get his attention. Rocco knows he is supposed to move over to the couch, put his arm around Karen, and ask, "What's wrong?" But he stays where he is.

Karen continues to "cry" for a few more minutes, then lowers her hand from her breast, raises her eyes, looks sorrowfully at Rocco, and says, "You're so cruel to me. You *always* blame me. I try so hard to please you and do what I think you want. I wore that sexy dress to the party tonight because I thought you like me to look good in front of your friends. Could I help it if one propositioned me? You embarrassed me so badly, I'll never be able to face any of them again. If I need to go out, I may do it at night or go to another town just so I won't have to face any of them. I don't know how much more I can take. I wish I were dead. Where are my pills? What you did has brought back my pain all over again."

Rocco knows he was upset over Karen's provocative behavior. From experience, he also knows where the conversation will go if he gets angry or apologetic. Instead, he says, "I must admit I became irritated when you started dancing so provocatively with one of the men at the party. You certainly became the center of attention. I knew your behavior was inappropriate, but rather than cause a scene there, I thought I would wait and talk to you about it at some point."

Never the one to take responsibility, Karen replies, "I thought you were attracted to me because of my outgoing personality. Now you condemn me for it. I don't know why you go to parties. You're always just standing around, not talking with anyone, just watching everyone else. When you do talk, it's so stilted, like you've never been around people before. At least I was able to get out and talk and laugh. At least *someone* noticed me! Why can't you be more human, have some feelings, and not be like a robot? You could have asked me to dance or gotten me a drink. You could have pushed your way in and got my attention. God knows, I've tried to bring out the man in you. Your friends are lots of fun. Not like you. What's wrong with a little flirting? Especially when your husband doesn't appreciate you. I was just having a little fun, but like all guys, you turn it immediately into something dirty and sexual. I try to give, to be open and friendly, but I'm always the used one to be thrown away and abused. Maybe if you gave me more attention, I wouldn't have to get noticed elsewhere."

Trying not to get defensive, Rocco says, "The issue is not me and how it's my fault for your doing what you do. The issue is your frequently pushing the limits with your behavior. I get the impression you try to taunt me into making a scene, like the caveman coming to claim his woman. I know I am very attentive to you. I have given up trying to figure out why you think you have to go to such extremes to get my attention. As much as it hurts me to say it, and I know it will hurt you too, your drama, your extremes, your threats have all got to stop. Keeping me always on my guard that something's going to happen is no way to treat someone you love. I feel baited many times. If I say nothing, I feel like a wuss, but if I say something to you, I come out of it feeling like everything's my fault. It's always a no-win situation for me."

THE TYPES OF PEOPLE WHO ARE MOST TRAPPED IN RELATIONSHIPS WITH HPDs

HPDs use all of the attention-seeking gifts they have to prey on us, and we normal human beings easily succumb to their allure or neediness. Caring people respond most to the role of helplessness that the HPD plays. The more sober and staid of us are prone to the HPD's charms, since frequently she presents in a refreshing and charming way that takes us out of the usual routine. HPDs can offer extraordinary changes to the usual pace of life. Men who are insecure with women find the attention of the HPD flattering and seductive.

However, in this category, the award primarily goes to the rescuer type whom the HPD exploits grandly. HPDs play right into the role of the needy (yet attractive and seemingly pliable) person in desperate search of help, especially in professional situations where the HPD will see the expert as her savior and will exploit your need (and role) to help for her own purposes.

Remember ————————————————————————————————

Any relationship with an HPD is an illusion based on whatever attention she is getting at the time. There is no depth, no intimacy . . . only misery.

Remember ————————————————————————————————

If it doesn't work, don't keep doing it!

SUMMARY

HPDs are very adaptable and can appeal to you in many ways—from being intellectually challenging to sexually provocative, or by appealing to your helping side by dramatically eliciting your sympathy. You are seduced one way or another to cater to the HPD's insatiable need to be the center of attraction.

CHAPTER **4**

The Smooth Operator: The Antisocial Personality Disorder (ASPD)

Charming, Beguiling, Captivating, and Cold

"Trust me. I would never lie to you."

K*ey point:* The bright antisocial personality disorder (ASPD) individual—frequently called the psychopath or sociopath—will control you with winning and charismatic behavior while conning and deceiving you. ASPDs are so good at what they do that they totally enrapture you (whether you are a man or a woman) before you recognize what is happening. They suck you in and suck you dry. This is Mr. or Ms. Slick, the very best salesperson you have ever encountered.

The less clever ASPD relies on baser skills of force and intimidation. This is the Thug, aggressive and forceful. With Mr. or Ms. Slick, you are *entranced* and used. With the Thug, you are *fearful* and used.

While people with other personality disorders seek to control and manipulate to get something (like attention) from you, the ASPD's main end is to control you. Having power over you is an end in itself. Invariably, the ASPD also wants something more tangible in terms of personal profit or pleasure—for example, money, a favor, or sex. Whatever an ASPD gets from you represents the hold he or she has over you and is secondary to the power.

ASPDs rely on deceit and lies. Disregarding the norms of society, ASPDs see themselves as unique, strong, and playing by their own rules. It is through these traits of alleged autonomy, self-directedness, charm, and

77

strength that the ASPD tries to influence you.

Although many ASPDs have found a home in prison because of a disregard for the law, many others have adeptly found a place in society in areas where they can successfully use people for their own ends. Since most of us tend not to associate with menacing felons like those portrayed on television (the Thug), we shall mostly deal with Mr. Slick, who may also have intimidating tendencies in physical or other ways. (For ease of discussion, we'll generally use the male pronoun throughout this chapter to refer to ASPDs, even though people of both genders exhibit this personality disorder). You might meet an ASPD in virtually every aspect of life, including lawyers, doctors, clergy, police, scoutmasters, stockbrokers, or simply the cherubic choirboy next door.

Red-Flag Feelings in You

Strongly drawn in by their magnetism
Dismissing your better judgment

Remember

The ASPD uses guile and deceit to charm you into his agenda. The more rapt you feel, the more wary you should be.

Picture This

Who Are the ASPDs You Might See?

The salesperson claiming his product—the car, the aluminum siding, the boat, the refrigerator—has *no* flaws or defects, will last forever, and will do much more than promised. He will answer all of your questions with what you want to hear rather than the truth.

Your business partner, defrauding you while saying you are to blame.

The attorney using clients' funds.

The antique dealer selling reproductions as authentic.

The politician with empty promises and full pockets.

The fellow whose favorite line when asked to admit to past misdeeds is "That's what they say."

The medical patient whom you have not seen in many months and who has not paid her bill but is now telephoning in a request for more pain pills.

The client who asks you to sign off falsely on some form—for example, for his disability—because he needs the money and the government can afford it.

The guy who cuts in front of you in a line and, if you object, says, "Want to take this out back and settle it?"

The woman who borrows something (for example, your money or your car) and never pays you back or returns the item. If she does, the property is damaged and not in the same condition in which you lent it.

The person who intrigues you because of individualism or the desire to beat the system. He is the investment guy who avoids taxes, the lawyer who bends the law, the man-killer who loves many and leaves many, or the wheeler-dealer business guy. They live life in the fast lane and captivate us with their tales of getting by while not obeying society's mundane rules. These are the rugged individualists or the intimidating entrepreneurs who capture our imagination and appeal to our admiration of the lone individual striking out against the system.

Remember

The ASPD is not around simply to tell you stories or to entertain. He does not need your attention. He wants something more from you.

Picture This

Professional Life

The biggest and most typically recurring mistake that you, as a professional, would make in dealing with the ASPD is believing that your experience and intelligence will keep you astute and out of the clutches of this manipulator. Professionals who deal frequently with ASPDs usually are most adroit, but even they fall prey to an ASPD's tricks. In your office, Mr. Smooth will indeed be smooth, smiling, and personable. He will have charmed your assistant or receptionist (has he hinted of a date or something else he could do for her out of the kindness of his heart?). This is the well-dressed, well-coiffed fellow who can sell ice to the Eskimos, sand to the Arabs, and American wine to the French. After talking his way in for an audience, he might convince the pope to convert to Buddhism or sell Queen Elizabeth a new palace. If not elegantly attired, he will still sport that platinum smile and warmth that will win you over immediately as someone you can trust and admire. Even though it is your office, somehow he is in charge. And you may likely not mind his taking over because of the fellow's winning ways and entertaining quality. He is at the same time one of the guys and someone who stands out in the crowd.

As he grasped the gold cross at his neck, one ASPD told a professional, "I speak from the heart, man to man." He was the model of sincerity and helpfulness. He then went on to give the professional tips on women, boats, cars, and bribery. The ASPD is Mr. Personality. If you were not dealing with him in a professional capacity, you might consider him to be one of those interesting people with whom you'd like to spend more time. He could even suggest doing something away from your stuffy office confines. He might even be able to do something for *you*.

In seeking an appointment with you, whatever persona he is portraying—from business leader, husband, troubled soul, big-game hunter, or man of the world—the ASPD conveys warmth and enthusiasm. How can you not trust him?

Remember

Never *trust an ASPD*.

An ASPD who is late for an appointment always has a plausible reason. Once you meet him, you forget his being late, for he is a charmer. Among the topics he'll bring up are:

- Whatever he thinks you want to hear.
- Whatever flatters your ego.
- Some topic he knows will seduce you (power, money, or sex).

READER/CUSTOMER CARE SURVEY

We care about your opinions! Please take a moment to fill out our online Reader Survey at **http://survey.hcibooks.com.**
As a **"THANK YOU"** you will receive a **VALUABLE INSTANT COUPON** towards future book purchases as well as a **SPECIAL GIFT** available only online! Or, you may mail this card back to us and we will send you a copy of our exciting catalog with your valuable coupon inside.
(PLEASE PRINT IN ALL CAPS)

First Name _____ MI. _____ Last Name _____

Address _____ City _____

State _____ Zip _____ Email _____

1. Gender
❏ Female ❏ Male

2. Age
❏ 8 or younger
❏ 9-12 ❏ 13-16
❏ 17-20 ❏ 21-30
❏ 31+

3. Did you receive this book as a gift?
❏ Yes ❏ No

4. Annual Household Income
❏ under $25,000
❏ $25,000 - $34,999
❏ $35,000 - $49,999
❏ $50,000 - $74,999
❏ over $75,000

5. What are the ages of the children living in your house?
❏ 0 - 14 ❏ 15+

6. Marital Status
❏ Single
❏ Married
❏ Divorced
❏ Widowed

7. How did you find out about the book?
(please choose one)
❏ Recommendation
❏ Store Display
❏ Online
❏ Catalog/Mailing
❏ Interview/Review

8. Where do you usually buy books?
(please choose one)
❏ Bookstore
❏ Online
❏ Book Club/Mail Order
❏ Price Club (Sam's Club, Costco's, etc.)
❏ Retail Store (Target, Wal-Mart, etc.)

9. What subject do you enjoy reading about the most?
(please choose one)
❏ Parenting/Family
❏ Relationships
❏ Recovery/Addictions
❏ Health/Nutrition
❏ Christianity
❏ Spirituality/Inspiration
❏ Business Self-help
❏ Women's Issues
❏ Sports

10. What attracts you most to a book?
(please choose one)
❏ Title
❏ Cover Design
❏ Author
❏ Content

TAPE IN MIDDLE; DO NOT STAPLE

IιιIIιιιIIιιIιιIιIιιIιιIιIIIιIιιIιιIιιιIιIιIιιIιI

FOLD HERE

Comments

- How all men are brothers (or, if it's woman-to-woman, how all women are part of the sisterhood) and need to help each other.
- Something or someone working against him.
- What he needs from you.

The ASPD is the consummate salesperson, but without an ounce of true kindness, concern, or remorse. His consulting with you goes beyond the typical client or patient seeking your expertise and recommendations. The ASPD exhibits an implicit disregard of the law or social rules. Therefore, whatever he is seeking from you, there is always an ulterior motive, a hidden agenda beyond the obvious. For example, if you are a physician and the ASPD wants to be placed on disability, his goal will be not only being placed on disability but also how he might worsen the disability (if it exists) or extend the time out. If he is in pain, he comes to you not just to relieve the pain, but also to get strong pills (perhaps narcotics) that he might sell later. If you are a social worker and you are involved with evaluating him in a child custody battle, he will want you not only to favor him for custody, but also to help him further discredit and defame his wife as much as possible. If the issue is legal in nature, he will be looking beyond his legal involvements (because, of course, he is absolutely innocent) and seeking what lawsuits he can bring against his libelous accusers.

His initial conversations will revolve around standard requests within your field. The ASPD will then ask you to venture into gray legal or ethical areas where he will try to cajole you into bending the rules. He does this by smoothly taking you out of your objective consultant role and making you his ally, his friend—two people fighting for what is good (for him).

Remember

ASPDs firmly believe that you are corruptible. They will take pleasure in bringing you over to the dark side, where they can control you. They will use every skill they have to accomplish this end.

As with other people with personality disorders whom you will see in a professional situation, you must have as much factual and objective information about the individual ASPD as possible, because ASPDs will gloss over anything negative that crops up in your examination or interview. The ASPD will rationalize or even lie to you, to the point of refuting established facts. A favorite response to negative information about him is his saying, "That's what they say." In this way, he does not deny whatever you've stated, but rather he implies that something is strongly amiss with others. The exchange will go something like this:

Professional: "It says here that you battered your wife on two occasions, had several affairs, and lost your job because you were stealing."

ASPD: "That's what they say."

Professional: "What do you say? Is this true?"

ASPD: "With all this women's lib stuff still around, everyone feels sorry for the wife, and we guys don't get a fair shake anymore."

Professional: "That's not answering the question. Did you beat your wife? Did you fool around? Did you steal?"

ASPD: "That sweet woman? I think it was her friends who told her to say that. I don't know where she got those bruises. Maybe she did it to herself. You know how women are. Yeah, when I wasn't getting anything at home, I did have a few affairs and even had a few kids, but it was only for the sex. I wasn't involved; she wanted the kids, not me. As far as work goes, that bastard had it in for me from the beginning. These people all are lying. Trust me, I always try to do the right thing. As a guy, you can understand that."

Remember ————————————————————————

Deception is a necessary part of the behavior. If he is good at what he does, you will not realize that you are being deceived, so be prepared.

If a spouse, the court, some agency, another client/patient, or a colleague refers an ASPD to you, be especially wary. Whoever sends him over to be evaluated may have a definite idea about the ASPD's manipulative ways and needs further confirmation of some sort (for example, a wife needs to confirm whether her lying, cheating husband is truly hopeless; the court desires to confirm he is malingering vs. some other psychiatric problem). However, do not assume that the referral source knows about this individual's manipulative power. It may be just the opposite—that the referrer was taken in and is sending him on to you so might also help out. ASPDs are adept at using a group of people to attain their ends.

Remember

You do not matter. *What* does *matter is what he can get from you.*

True Life

True-Life Adventure 1:
Mendacious Mike and Dr. Bob

Mike's wife of several years made an appointment with Dr. Bob, a psychiatrist, to evaluate and treat (if possible) her husband for his perpetual lying. When she made the appointment, Mike's wife left information that Mike was only coming to the appointment under her threat of divorce. Mike had married into money, was a sports jock from college, and had held jobs as the golf pro at various country clubs for short terms. Mike usually lost his job because of his laziness, stealing, and/or getting too chummy with the female members. His lying had reached the masters' level, with his wife unable to trust him as to where he would be, who he was with, when he would be home, and what he did with their (her) money. She also suspected he was using drugs along with his drinking, and he may have been supplying some club members with drugs as well.

Dr. Bob: "Well, Mike, what are you doing here?"

Mike: "You know, my wife made this appointment and forced me to come. She's again bringing up divorcing me if I don't do things her way. She's always moody and very controlling. She thinks she can get away with it since she holds the purse strings. You gotta agree that no woman should treat a man that way, and that no real man should let her do it."

Dr. Bob: "'Do things her way'? What does that mean?"

Mike: "You know, be at her beck and call."

Dr. Bob: "It seems to me there was something about your lying to her a lot."

Mike: "Yeah, I do lie a lot, but I do it not to hurt her. If I tell her the things I'm involved with, she'll only get upset and hurt. Better not to tell her and keep peace."

Dr Bob: "So you're lying to her because you care about her. Do I have that straight?"

Mike: "Yeah, I do care for her . . . and her money doesn't hurt either." Scott laughs and gives a knowing wink to Dr. Bob.

Mike then goes on to talk about his golden college days, playing golf now, his sexual conquests, his speeding tickets, his run-ins with the law for suspected drug use and dealing, his affairs (his wife's fault), the bounced checks, and his pilfering money from their account and hiding it from her. He shows no remorse or guilt for his behavior and explains it away as necessary for him to do ("self-protection," as he calls it) to maintain his lifestyle.

Mike: "She's got a lot of money. It's not like she misses it. She wasn't the best-looking babe around when I married her. In a way, I figured I did her (and her family) a favor by walking down the aisle with her.

"You have to understand. She knew I was this way when she married me. I told her I wasn't about to change, so she knew what she was getting into. Now she wants it otherwise. Say, Doc, do you play golf? You look like a five-handicap.

"I'm not a bad person. If I took advantage of some people, they brought it on themselves. Only the strong survive. Are you married, Doc?"

Dr. Bob: "Yes, and, by the way, my handicap is nine. I can't seem to putt well."

Mike grins. "You ought to swing by the club sometime, and maybe I can look at your style."

Dr. Bob becomes more sympathetic as Mike talks on about his moody, demanding wife who will not accept him as he is. Mike first jokes and then more seriously asks Dr. Bob if he now has to talk with his wife. Dr. Bob says he will talk with her if she calls. Then Mike asks Dr. Bob, "I certainly do not want you to lie or say anything you do not believe, but could you say that I don't have any serious problems and that it is her paranoia?"

Mike then again offers Dr. Bob some free golf tips sometime in the future with another wink and a nod. In Mike's mind, here they are, Mike and Dr. Bob, two guys commiserating with each other about moody, controlling women.

At the end of the appointment when he is asked to pay the bill, Mike says, "Bill me." However, when she made the appointment, his wife was told that he would need to pay cash for obvious reasons, and she had promised to make sure Mike had the money. When retold he was to pay then and there, Mike becomes indignant and says, "What's the matter, don't you guys trust me? I came here in good faith to get some help. Now you challenge my integrity. How can that be therapeutic? It only tears down my self-esteem."

With the thought of some future free golf lessons and lowering his handicap, Dr. Bob apologizes to Mike for upsetting and humiliating him and tells his secretary to bill him. Mike leaves the office with a big smile.

Remember

ASPDs have no remorse or guilt for their actions. When they do admit to doing something against someone else, it is the other person's fault for being dumb. "If he lets me take his money, how am I to blame?"

True Life

True-Life Adventure 2:
Very Slick Rick and Frank, Social Worker

Rick's wife was divorcing him, and the court demanded that he see the social worker, Frank, because Rick was contesting child custody going to his wife. Rick was rarely home, spent little time with his two children, and when he did see his children, he was irresponsible (letting them drink his beer, wander away, or do dangerous things at the playground). Rick had held jobs for short periods, relied on his wife's working, and had a past prison record for dealing drugs. He told Frank, "Some loser ratted me out. Otherwise, I never would have been caught."

Rick is a very handsome man in his early forties with wavy, dark brown hair, piercing blue eyes, and an incredibly solid body. He has a radiant smile and is immediately likeable from the warmth that emanates from his personality. He is an articulate, smooth talker.

Rick instantly starts off by talking about himself without prompting from the social worker. He claims to do five hundred push-ups a day to keep "solid." Rick says, "I'm like steel. I wanted to show my wife what a real man was." He dismisses his affairs and says, "A man has his needs, and she doesn't like sex anyway." Rick describes his many sexual escapades at length to Frank, as he assumes that Frank will be impressed with his conquests.

Rick had been a professional dancer at one point in his life. He tells Frank, "I would give lessons to the ladies, and they loved it. We would be doing the tango, and I would lock our hips together. I gave them the sensation . . . like a peppermint patty!"

Encouraged by Frank, Rick talked on. "I remember a blonde once. I met her at a bar I would go to on the bay when I had my cigarette boat. I'd cruise by and check out how many rich, divorcées were sitting at the bar. Then I would slowly move the boat in and tie it up as I flexed my muscles all of the time. So, this blonde, she was dressed all in black . . . like Catwoman. I took care of her. She was the cat, and I was the cat-*nip*." When Rick later learned the blonde was one of his child's teachers, he said, "Man, did that give me a rush. Doin' my son's teacher."

Believing that he had now sufficiently awed Frank, Rick says, "Look, Doc, I want to be totally honest with you. I don't really want custody of the kids. But this witch-wife of mine is looking to screw me out of my money. I did hide some away when I was dealing drugs, and she knows about it. A guy has to look after himself, you know, and I don't want that witch to get anything. She never behaved like a real woman anyhow." Rick pleads, "I want to use this custody issue as a bargaining chip with her. Can you help me out? You know how unreasonable women can get. You must see it all of the time in your job. I don't know how you do what you do. I certainly couldn't. Let's let her think that I might get custody, and that might make her back down about the money."

Rick goes on, "The other thing you could help me with is maybe getting her declared unfit. When I was in jail, she took some tranquilizers for a time and saw a counselor. Is there any way I could use that against her? Whaddaya say, Doc?"

Remember

The manipulation in this example may seem obvious. The smoother and brighter ASPD will not be so obvious. When you find yourself being seduced by the charm and about to bend the rules or to do a favor, be very careful. You will know this is happening when you need to talk yourself into a behavior or action you might not otherwise undertake.

True Life

True-Life Adventure 3:
Perfidious Pete and the Cautious College Counselor

Pete is in his second year of college and continues to have difficulties academically. He squeaked by in the first year but now is on probation. Pete likely has an alcohol problem, with his partying going way beyond that of his classmates. Pete is failing all of his classes, which he rarely attends. He spends his time drinking, playing cards, and hustling coeds, and maybe selling some drugs here and there.

The college counselor asks to see Pete to discuss his situation. The counselor is expecting to speak with someone who has a bad and indignant attitude, but the counselor is surprised to find Pete almost charismatic.

Pete, with a huge smile, enters the office. He says, "This is a great office. Plenty of sunshine, and the things you've decorated with are outstanding. This place has a lot of class. Were you ever an interior decorator?"

Counselor: "Thanks, but, you know, we're here to talk about you. You are about to be asked to leave the college."

Pete replies, "I know. But I did want to tell you how much this office impresses me. A room can tell so much about a person."

Now turning grim, Pete says, "I know. I know. I have been seriously bad about classes and my grades. I get behind, and then it gets me so depressed that I get further behind. My mom has been sick, and my dad out of work. I wonder if he's not depressed too, or even suicidal. I worry so much about them. I should be doing better, if only for them. But those things shouldn't be excuses. Are your parents alive?"

As she is about to answer about herself, the counselor thinks better of it and says, "I didn't know there were problems at home."

Pete: "Yeah. I think it's my worry that makes me do what I do. I'm just trying to run away from it."

The counselor and Pete talk on about his situation, with Pete affirming his resolution to change his ways. At the end of the meeting, he asks, "Is there any way I can get out of taking midterms? Because of the family situation?" As the counselor is about to consider this request, the light bulb goes on. She tells him she'll get back to him and later checks into Pete's family situation. She finds that Pete's mom is as healthy as she could be. Pete's dad is out of work, but it's because the dad retired early with a huge income. The dad may be depressed only in trying to figure out how to spend all of his money.

Pete, accusing the counselor of lying and misunderstanding what he said, is asked to leave school.

Remember

ASPDs glow with deceit and irresponsibility. They will flatter you and try to get you to disclose things about yourself that they might then use to manipulate you. They will change things around and try to get you to align with them against something. You need to keep to the points, being clear and straightforward. Always make good on threats or consequences, or you will otherwise be seen as weak and exploitable. And never talk about yourself. Repeat: Never talk about yourself.

Picture This

Business Life

Mr. Slick is everywhere in the business world because there are so many situations to be exploited for fun and profit. ASPDs in the corporate environment are well-mannered, well-groomed, well-educated individuals who muscle their way in less physical ways than the Thug, but who are nonetheless forceful. The business world is a fertile breeding ground for the politically adept scam artist, the self-promoting egotist, and the manipulative player. You come across the ASPD wherever someone can be exploited, including the fields of medicine, law and law enforcement, politics, religion, academia, sales, construction, and so on.

Some areas of the business world encourage risk taking, shallowness, and backstabbing while being unemotional in the process. Business can and often is about money (profit margins), power (control of market share or taking advantage of the competition), and possibly a bit of sex thrown in, although money and power are often more arousing.

The business sections of many stores are filled with books on leadership and success within the corporate world, right next to books on how to make your million dollars. All are usually written in positive and glowing terms about the subject: getting ahead in business. Curiously, the darker side of business is less discussed, in spite of the fact that sometimes the most aggressive, unruly, ruthless, and cold individuals rise to the top in companies that actually foster this behavior.

In business, the ASPD is found in all areas where people or a system can be exploited, even at the lower levels where people are in a job for the quick scam or to move up in the system where better pickings are.

ASPDs are not team players. They tend to flaunt authority and traditional rules, and they impress others as being independent thinkers with their antagonistic and highly competitive style often viewed as pluses within a company. Therefore, ASPDs show up in areas of business that might promote out-of-the-box thinking or less conventional methods of making money. These are the entrepreneurs, fast risers in the corporation, or independent businessmen.

Remember —————————————————————————————

ASPDs are in it only for themselves.

Among the types of people who are often ASPDs:

- The aggressive and yet admired self-made man who exploits others, reneges on deals, and is renowned for his cool and calculating demeanor.
- The academic who plagiarizes others' work, has affairs with the higher-ups' wives, and then blackmails the guys not to reveal their wives' transgressions.

True Life

True-Life Adventure 1:
Jumping Jerry

Jerry is in his late twenties and has held several positions before coming to his new company. He is unclear as to why he changed jobs other than "it was the thing to do." Jerry appears very friendly with one of the senior managers. In meetings, Jerry usually makes remarks that sound aggressive and incisive but which generally lack substance. He always talks around a subject, demeans traditional approaches and plans, and then is sarcastic to anyone who might question him. The rumor is that Jerry keeps one jump ahead of being fired but seems to charm his way into employment. Jerry has made it a priority to learn everyone's function in the office so that he can determine how to use him or her. He is difficult to pin down about anything. Jerry dates various secretaries of the higher-up people, and then dumps them after he gets certain information from them. He shrugs this off as just doing business.

Remember

ASPDs frequently go from job to job. They stay just long enough to get whatever they want. They never take a job for the long haul. ASPDs want quick results and manipulate whomever is necessary to obtain them. To ASPDs, everyone is a sucker to be used.

True Life

True-Life Adventure 2:
Dr. Smooth and Dr. Bob

Dr. Bob, a psychiatrist, was at one time the medical director of a large mental health clinic that already had Dr. Smooth on the payroll when Dr. Bob came on board.

Dr. Smooth had acquired a reputation as being efficient in handling emergencies and having no tolerance for patients who had substance-abuse issues. For Dr. Smooth, no drug user could also have a severe mental illness.

As a result, he dismissed many patients without treatment and with the statement, "Come back with six months of sobriety behind you, and I *may* help you out." Many patients who had had long-standing psychiatric problems, like depression, along with their drug or alcohol problems complained, with Dr. Bob having to speak repeatedly with Dr. Smooth about his brash and seemingly callous attitude. Dr. Slick was unmoved and simply said he found these patients malingerers not worthy of his expertise. Dr. Bob was curious about this attitude since rumors were afloat that Dr. Smooth frequently wrote prescriptions for other patients (who were usually young, busty, and attractive) for large amounts of tranquilizers, pain medications, and diet pills. Dr. Smooth denied this and said, "I would never do that. Show me the evidence."

Also during the time of his employment, Dr. Smooth, a handsome, muscular, and quite charming man (married with three children), had been known to be having affairs with numerous young women who worked at the clinic. Dr. Bob was neither handsome nor muscular. He both envied Dr. Smooth for his facile way with women while also having concerns that Dr. Smooth might bring about a harassment suit against himself and the center. When Dr. Bob discussed his concerns, Dr. Smooth, with a big smile, said, "If they want me, what can I do? I'm just *spreading love*. I have no worries about any of this coming back to bite me. What I do is get all of the women to write me love notes. Look here in my desk drawer, I have letters from all of them expressing their love and sexual things they want to do. If ever any one of them files a complaint, I'll have her letter as proof that she was very willing."

Dr. Smooth had no concerns about his wife learning about his behavior and was casual in describing how he constantly lied to her. Conventional and risk-adverse, Dr. Bob recognized that a part of him admired Dr. Smooth's reckless and nonchalant attitude. Dr Bob knew he should be firing Dr. Smooth, but, despite many concerns, he tried to work with him.

One day, a pharmacist called the clinic to report that one of the clinic's employees, a friend of Dr. Smooth, had attempted to forge prescriptions for narcotics by signing Dr. Smooth's name. Initially, Dr. Smooth was indignant that his friend would betray him like this. "I would have given her the prescription, if she had asked me," he asserted.

After the clinic investigated what had happened, the rumors appeared to be true. It seems that Dr. Smooth had been prescribing numerous prescriptions for many employees for narcotics for many months. He also was prescribing narcotics for a few close friends outside of the clinic.

When confronted, Dr. Smooth was calm and cool. He claimed that such behavior was rampant among all of the doctors at the clinic (untrue), that the staff sought him out, and that he was doing them and the clinic a favor. ("They wouldn't have to give up a day's work to go and see a doctor for a prescription.") "Besides," he said, "They asked for the prescriptions. It wasn't like I was pushing things on them."

Dr. Smooth also pointed out that the clinic did not have a firm policy forbidding writing of prescriptions for nonpatients. Dr. Smooth's opinion was that the situation was the clinic's fault, despite the fact that a state law forbade writing narcotics prescriptions for nonpatients.

Dr. Bob, knowing now how much he had been lied to and feeling like an idiot, was savoring firing Dr. Smooth. This did not happen, however, since Dr. Smooth abruptly resigned to take another job that he had been seeking behind the clinic's back. He told his new employers, who did not check his references because he was too good to be true, that he needed to make a clean break because he was too pressured at the clinic. Dr. Smooth eventually had his medical license placed on probation for five years for indiscriminately prescribing narcotics. He continued to affirm his innocence.

Remember ——————————————————————————————————

ASPDs have no conscience. They see themselves as victims and absolve themselves from blame. They are very smooth.

True Life

True-Life Adventure 3:
Treacherous Ted

Ted acquired his medical technician job in a small hospital by demonstrating his enthusiasm and affable personality. He could have easily charmed his way into a job in any organization. Ted rapidly made friends at the hospital and sized up everyone. There were those who would have influence to help him, those who would do his bidding, and those of whom he must be wary.

Ted cultivated the higher-ups in the administration when they came around, especially the administrator and the head nurse. He made sure that they noticed him as he engaged them in pleasant conversation. He seduced others around him with promises of prestige, more money, security, a relationship, or attention. All of these things would occur when he moved up. All who knew Ted saw someone who always had some deal going, like running the football pool or getting tickets for a concert. He might ask for your money for the tickets before the purchase and never give you an accounting, but people let it go since he was such a good guy. He might borrow money and delay paying it back with the words, "I'm good for it. Come on, don't you trust me?"

By using those higher-ups he cultivated and his lackeys to whom he had promised the world, Ted moved from being a technician to assistant administrator to head administrator of his area in six months. Ted had reached a level of success by manipulation and cunning. By this time, anyone who spoke disparagingly of him was not thought of well. "How could such a great guy be perceived in such a foul way?" said one of the senior managers, now one of Ted's golfing buddies.

Ted was let go when it was discovered that he was stealing hospital supplies and patients' belongings, and dealing drugs to other workers. Later, people discovered the large amounts of money he had borrowed from many of them and never paid back.

Remember

ASPDs thrive on deceit. They con others and are untroubled by such things as loyalty or guilt.

True Life

True-Life Adventure 4:
Ben, the Investment Advisor

Ben was referred to Earl by a friend because "Ben really knows how to wheel and deal in the market." Earl's friend told him, "If there's a way of making a buck, Ben will know how." Despite the fact that Earl allowed Ben to handle his investments over the last few years, Earl was leery of him for some unspecified reason.

Ben would say, "Trust me to take care of your money, I know best." But Earl wondered when Ben spoke in broad terms when asked about his investment strategies, or when he smiled and frequently changed the subject when asked about various service charges on the account, or why it was difficult to get a full listing of the account's activities. Earl postponed a more direct confrontation since Ben had made Earl some money over the years.

Ben always responded, "Don't worry about all those figures. It's the bottom line you should be interested in. Let *me* worry about the little stuff. Haven't I made money for you?"

Then the news broke about Ben's nasty divorce. Ben's soon-to-be-ex-wife revealed his flair for persistent buying and selling from clients' accounts to generate commissions for himself, his "borrowing" money from accounts to pay for his drug habit, his mistresses, and his secret accounts used to hide money from her and the IRS.

Ben had involved some of his investors in some of his less-than-legal dealings. In order to save himself, he now threatened to expose them for their involvement with him. Despite this, Ben's wife expressed her concern: "He's so charming and likeable, I don't think anyone will believe me about what a liar and cheat he is. His golfing buddies won't. And I wonder if the people he's made money for, even though he's ripped them off, will think ill of him. They like their money."

Remember ————————————————————————

The ASPD is reckless and disregards social norms. If you are involved with one, expect that you are breaking the law somewhere. When you start to support someone's unethical/illegal activities, be wary that you have been sucked in. Also, expect him to turn on you if it suits his needs.

Picture This

Personal Life

You might wonder why anyone would stay involved with another who coldly manipulates, cheats, and uses you repeatedly and has no guilt over it. We usually get involved with ASPDs initially by either admiring their physical power (the Thug) or being seduced by Mr. Slick's aura. The Thug entrances some as a result of his aggressiveness and the control he appears to exert over others. He may not be as smooth as Mr. Slick, but the Thug attracts people by his primitive power and ability to intimidate others. At first, there is excitement over the Thug's behavior, until the intimidation turns on you. Then you may be too scared to leave.

Mr. Slick is smooth of tongue, glib, and clever, and he jokes and has a wonderful personality. He has an aura that singles him out from other men. He tells you what you want to hear. He beguiles you with promises of happiness, money, or whatever he thinks you want. Even when he fails to deliver, he continues to charm. Who can resist?

In general, people in personal relationships with ASPDs find them irresponsible and not to be trusted. Rarely do they meet marital, parental, or financial obligations. ASPDs give affection only to manipulate. When confronted, they frequently become debasing, dominating, and vengeful.

Remember ————————————————————————

The ASPD wants to control you, and he will seek out your weaknesses to do this.

True Life

True-Life Adventure 1:
Fast Eddie and Sharon

Sharon knew Fast Eddie from the high school they attended in an upper-class suburb. Although popular and attractive, Sharon was not in the really "in" crowd in which Fast Eddie ran. He was one of the most popular guys in school. He was the student government president and homecoming king . . . and he looked great in a tux. Fast Eddie was president of a number of student organizations, getting elected on his good looks and personality. He reminded Sharon of the Eddie Haskell character from *Leave It to Beaver.* The TV kid always had the right thing to say, although the Fast Eddie she knew was much smoother and more believable in his delivery.

It was rumored that Fast Eddie had had sex not only with one of the younger teachers but also with one of his friends' mothers. Fast Eddie might also have been involved in other mischief in school (selling exams and stealing computer equipment), but somehow he was able to talk his way out of these problems, along with help from his wealthy father. These things only seemed to excite Sharon when she thought of Fast Eddie, who always had something nice to say to her, even though they never dated. Fast Eddie appeared to her as an adventurous and carefree individual who was not bound by the more mundane rules of society. His charm justified his behaviors.

After graduation, both Sharon and Fast Eddie went to college. Sharon went to an Ivy League school and Fast Eddie to a local college since his grades were mediocre. At their five-year reunion, Sharon and Fast Eddie struck up a new relationship, with Sharon taken again by Fast Eddie's cheerful and light-hearted personality. They were married three months later, with Sharon swept off her feet by promises of undying love, wealth, and happiness. At the time, Fast Eddie was doing very well selling Mercedes at the local dealership. After their baby was born, Sharon kept her job at Fast Eddie's urgings since the car market could be so variable and he had already changed jobs three times in the past year. Fast Eddie always justified his leaving places by saying, "You can't fly like an eagle when you work with turkeys."

One day, Sharon arrived home early to find Fast Eddie's demo Mercedes parked in the driveway. She found her husband in bed with the babysitter, a local college girl. The baby was screaming in the next room. Fast Eddie, lying there naked, loudly denied that anything happened. He then claimed that he had innocently stopped home to check on the baby, and that the coed seduced him.

After much soul-searching, Sharon divorced Fast Eddie. In the divorce battle, he sued Sharon for support, maintaining that he had no income, although he was being paid under the table. Fast Eddie portrayed Sharon as a greedy, promiscuous, always serious, and never-at-home wife, while he was the wholesome mate. Sharon received custody of the child, but continued to return to court, trying to get Fast Eddie to pay the alimony and child support she was awarded.

Remember

ASPDs lie and cheat. They have no emotional depth or caring. "Losers deserve to lose" would be the extent of their passion. Ivy League educations do not protect you from people with ASPD. They play on your emotions, not your brains.

True Life

True-Life Adventure 2:
Dancing Dan and Marsha

Dan is a successful stockbroker. Marsha had been in investment banking and met Dan through some business dealings. Dan was the consummate salesman. Although she knew he had a reputation as a womanizer, Marsha allowed herself to be entranced by Dan and let herself believe that she was the special woman for whom he would change. They married and lived well, with a big house and nice cars.

Because of her job Marsha frequently worked late, so Dan's erratic hours never became an issue until Marsha's job changed and she was home at more regular times. Then she became more aware of Dan's frequent late-night "dinners with clients" and his drinking.

On occasion when he was drunk, Dan would tell Marsha about how he frequently would buy and sell stocks in the various accounts he managed in order to generate commissions for himself. He bragged to her about the insider trading he did and the money he made for himself and selected friends. Marsha, the more conventional banker-type, was further shocked to hear how Dan and his boss cooked the books to make it appear that Dan was making much less income than he does. "It's my American duty to cheat the IRS," Dan would assert.

But it was mostly the womanizing that soured Marsha, as Dan began doing it more blatantly. The final straw occurred when Marsha learned she had herpes, given to her by her wandering husband.

When she discussed divorce with an attorney, many of whom could not take on Marsha as a client because they were friends of Dan, Marsha learned her sad state: The house was heavily mortgaged and there were high loans on the cars. Furthermore, Dan had hidden much of the savings, reported a meager income, and would probably go after her for support.

Remember

Relationships with ASPDs are superficial and usually short because nothing of substance keeps them going. The relationship only endures if the other person is willing to be miserable with the lying and deceit.

DISCUSSION

ASPDs are the sweet talkers, the self-assured storytellers, the persuasive charmers, and the seemingly brilliant self-made men. They run the gamut from businesspeople, police officers, or professionals to the personable waiter or bartender who smiles his way into a bigger tip, then steals your credit card number. These types of ASPDs appeal to you in a more positive way, while others appeal to more primitive emotions. The latter types of ASPDs attract some people with their physical selves. They can be intimidating or threatening with their physical aura and use these behaviors to manipulate you. ASPDs and psychopaths are the same.

ASPDs primarily seek to control and exploit you without any concerns about your rights. Although this is true for most personality disorders, it is especially so with ASPDs, who have no respect for fairness and social norms.

The DSM-IV (*The Diagnostic and Statistical Manual of Mental Disorders,* Fourth Edition) describes ASPDs as having a pervasive pattern of disregard for and violation of the rights of others, occurring since age fifteen, and having three (or more) of the following characteristics:

- A failure to conform to social norms with respect to lawful behaviors as indicated by repeatedly performing acts that are grounds for arrest.
- Deceitfulness as indicated by repeated lying, use of aliases, or conning others for personal profit or pleasure.
- Impulsivity or failure to plan ahead.
- Irritability and aggressiveness as indicated by repeated physical fights or assaults.
- A reckless disregard for the safety of others.
- Consistent irresponsibility as indicated by repeated failure to sustain consistent work behavior or honor financial obligations.
- A lack of remorse as evidenced by being indifferent or rationalizing having hurt, mistreated, or stolen from another.
- Evidence of problems with conduct before age fifteen.

Breaking rules once in a while is not uncommon. You may speed, take a longer lunch break, tell a white lie, not tell a salesperson that she undercharged you, not look for the owner of the twenty dollars you found, or take something from the office. Some may even go further in breaking the rules by cheating on a spouse, participating in some unethical business practices, or inflating expenses on your income tax. Most of the time, our conscience or our fears of getting caught keep us in line. If we do engage in something wrong and get caught, the experience usually hits home and prevents us from repeating the wrong. *What separates ASPDs is that they have no conscience.* The smart ones only learn improved methods for getting away with things, while the dumber ones just keep making the same mistakes over and over and landing in jail. Not surprisingly, a large percentage of ASPDs are found in prison. If the ASPD in prison changes his ways, it is never from remorse but rather from the insight that his behavior keeps getting him in trouble, so his behavior has to change because it is no longer in his own best interest.

ASPDs, as with all individuals with personality disorders, have respect for your values or you only insofar as they can use you. ASPDs, however, will often break the law (and certainly skirt the law) in how they manipulate. Their only goal is: "What's in it for me." A person with antisocial personality disorder is a scammer, a user, and a manipulator.

We all think we can easily recognize this particular type of person and deal with him or her. In reality, few of us are really adept at dealing with ASPDs.

Remember ────────────────────────────────

ASPDs spend their lives doing what they do. They devote much effort to refining their skills in how to manipulate others. More often than not, the ASPD, like the confidence man who shares this behavior, uses us and we do not even know it. If we are aware of being used by the master ASPD, what is astounding is that we will rationalize the experience because the ASPD is such a charmer: "He's a good guy, I don't begrudge him the extra commission."

───

ASPDs play on basic human emotions. They flatter your ego or entice you with power or wealth or perhaps with something more intellectual like "us against the corrupt system." ASPDs look for your weaknesses. They observe your behavior and cleverly draw out your secret fantasies, your goals, and your desires, and then use them to manipulate you. Lines you might hear from an ASPD are as follows:

"Honey, I can make you a star."

"Your family deserves more."

"Doctor, insurance companies seem to control the country. The greedy bastards give you and me nothing but trouble. We can get back at them with your taking a stand and filling out the forms stating that I'm disabled."

"You deserve more money to spend on your family. Invest with me."

"Ms. Auditor, we can't allow this company to let so many people down. Your blowing the whistle will ruin so many lives."

Remember

ASPDs entice you by getting you to align with them. Once the two of you are bonded on some common path, an ASPD has control over you.

While the Mr. Slick type of ASPD charms his way through life and works on the periphery of the law, ASPDs with the thuggish type of behavior are generally the more irresponsible, reckless, and impulsive people who have run up against the law almost from early childhood. They do not hold on to jobs for long and do a poor job when employed. They lie, cheat, and abuse others more through intimidation than their allure, but many use both. Their relationships are superficial. They are aggressive and irritable, and often are involved with drugs and alcohol.

The cause of this personality disorder is unknown. However, a higher incidence of this problem occurs in those who have an ASPD parent. If your father is a user, he is likely to demonstrate to his offspring how to use people, and the ASPD's children then take up the family business.

By current estimates, men are three times more likely than women to have this disorder. Most of the time the official diagnosis of ASPD applies only to those who have had involvement with the law. This statistical approach likely decreases immensely the actual incidence of the disorder; as noted, the smarter ASPDs avoid the law while manipulating many others for their own gain. They have learned to work the system to exploit others.

Remember

ASPDs always want something from you, even though it seems like they are doing something for you. Their primary goal is: "What's in it for me?"

Even though they appear sociable and outgoing, ASPDs deep down are loners since they care only about themselves and have no desire to have real relationships. They believe that all people are untrustworthy and corruptible. They see the world as a predatory place where they must be the smarter predator. "Get them before they get me" is how they think, and in this fashion they justify their manipulative behavior. The pattern of ASPD behavior is to:

- More likely charm than threaten you.
- Feel you out for something they can manipulate in you.
- Charm some more.
- Get you to align with them . . . at which point you are lost to them.
- Use this bond to exploit you.

Remember

As with all personality disorders, first and foremost be aware of how the ASPD makes you feel. Use this awareness and knowledge to deal with him rather than being used and manipulated. People with personality disorders use your feelings to control you. ASPDs flatter or threaten you into doing something against your better judgment.

The Contrasts That Confuse You
How People with Antisocial Personality Disorder . . .

See Themselves	Want to Be Perceived
Visionary	Articulate
Self-driven	Independent
Charming	Captivating
Rugged individualist	Entertaining
His own man	Smooth
Highly focused	Power-driven
Caring	People pleaser
Warm	Successful
Influential	Commanding
Trustworthy	Adventurous
Convincing	Exciting
A man's man	A woman's man
Sensitive	Self-assured
Victimized	Wanting to share
Aggressive	Interested only in you
Nonconforming	Courageous
Superior	Upright

How ASPDs Will Appear to You if They Trap You

Articulate
Socially at ease
Convincing
Strong
Independent
Charming
Full of promise
Smooth
Powerful
Personable
Entertaining
Amusing
Exciting
Charismatic

Imaginative
Fascinating
Eloquent
Intriguing
Creative
Cool
Calculating
Commanding
Self-assured
Tenacious
Shrewd
Astute
Insightful

How ASPDs Should Appear to You if You Are *Not* Trapped by Them

Slick
Power-driven
Selfish
Conniving
Scheming
Wily
Devious
Dangerous
Manipulating
Elusive
Superficial
Amoral
Unethical

Remorseless
Deceitful
Unreliable
Always with a hidden agenda
Untrustworthy
Lying
Glib
Predatory
Rationalizing
Blameless
Self-centered
Ruthless
Callous

Remember ────────────────────────────

How do they make you feel?

A Typical Conversation with an ASPD: Dr. Bob and Conning Clyde

Dr. Bob rushes to return Clyde's urgent phone call. Clyde had seen Dr. Bob for only one appointment many months ago, during which Clyde requested some pain medication for recurring migraines. Clyde did not make a return appointment, nor follow up with some blood tests Dr. Bob ordered. Clyde, having given wrong insurance information, never paid his bill.

Dr. Bob: "Hi, Clyde. What can I do for you?"

Clyde: "Hello, Dr. Bob. I really appreciate your taking the time to give me a call back. Are you still dressing so well? I remember that fabulous suit you were wearing."

Dr. Bob: "Yes, I still try to dress well, but I have to be honest, my wife picks out many of my clothes."

Clyde: "You're a fortunate man to have such a great wife."

Dr. Bob: "Yes, I am. Clyde, is there something wrong? Your message said 'urgent.'"

Clyde: "When I was last in to see you, I was very impressed with how much you seemed to care about your patients. You appeared genuinely concerned about their suffering and how you might help them. I felt you were *really* interested in helping me. I felt exceptionally good when I left your office."

Dr. Bob: "Yes, I try to be as empathetic as possible to my patients' problems. Thanks for the compliment. They're so rare. People usually complain and are unappreciative."

Clyde: "I knew you were the person I could rely on. I have had some personal problems within my family and also have been involved in some stressful business dealings. As a result, my migraines have returned. I need a prescription for something stronger than you last ordered. Perhaps something with a narcotic base in it like other doctors have given me in the past. Your secretary said that I would have to come in to see you, but, and I know you'll understand this with your busy schedule, my time is very tight right now . . . and the pain is excruciating. Dr. Bob, I know you have your rules about this sort of thing, but could you make an exception and please call in a prescription? I'll be happy to make a future appointment when my schedule opens up. I know I still owe some money. I tried going for those lab tests, but the place was always closed when I went over. I'll try again tomorrow. My pain is taking away that quality time I spend with my family, and it is affecting my wife and my children, as well as business."

Typical Charmed Response to the ASPD

Dr. Bob: "Okay, Clyde, I'll call in a prescription this time if you'll promise to make that follow-up appointment and get the lab tests."

Clyde: "You can trust me to follow through on all of that. Thanks a lot. Would you please prescribe a hundred pills since it's cheaper that way? And maybe a few refills?"

How does the conversation make you feel? How could Dr. Bob, an accomplished physician, be such a complete boob? But we have all done this in one form or another. Think of the salesperson telling you how great you look in something, the car salesman telling you how much you deserve that car or the prestige you will gain by driving it, or the huckster promoting weight loss without diet or exercise. Have you ever gone out of your way to help a charming coworker and in the end felt dumb? The phrase "too good to be true" has merit for good reason.

Typical Angry Response to the ASPD

Dr. Bob: "What do you take me for, Clyde, a complete idiot? You didn't follow up with the lab tests I ordered, nor did you make another appointment with me . . . and you still owe me money. Now you call out of the blue and expect me to prescribe narcotics for you. You take up my valuable time with this nonsense."

How You Will Feel in Dealing with ASPDs

At first . . .

Charmed	"What a delightful, personable fellow."
Flattered	"I really like this guy."
Entertained	"Great stories."
Thrilled/excited	"I'm living in the fast lane! I'm finally taking a chance at something."

How You Will Feel in Dealing with ASPDs *(cont'd)*

Impressed	"He's done things I wish I could do. What a guy. . . . He's a nonconformist who lives by his own code."
Willing to bend the rules	"He makes a good point. Why shouldn't I do that?"

Later . . .

Suspicious	"Is he too good to be true?"
Confused	"He says one thing, then another."
Used	"I helped him out, and he just threw me away."
Abused	"He hurts me."
Ashamed	"I did *what*?"
Fearful	"He's manipulated people against me, and when I threatened to report him, he said he knew how to get even with me."
Taken in	"It made sense at the time. How dumb could I be?"
Intimidated	"He could hurt me (my job, my family, my reputation, etc.)."
Deceived	"The bastard lied to me."
Betrayed	"I thought he was sleeping only with me." "Where's my money?"
Overwhelmed	"It's all about power with him."
Guilty	"He said it was my fault that I let him use me."

One coworker of an ASPD remarked: "He joined our team at work and asked for my help. Now I see he was using me as a pawn to advance himself. He found out the people he had to guard against and avoided them. He kissed management's butt, lied about me to them, and took my job. Despite his smile, he was a cold manipulator. He told me once, 'Losers deserve to lose.' Of course, I thought he was talking about other people."

Remember ───────────────────────────────

ASPDs lie. If you think you are the only one who is getting the truth, you are deceiving yourself.

How to Deal with ASPDs

What You Cannot Do

- Think you are too smart to be taken in.
- Think you are something special to him.
- Expect him to change for you.
- Align, bond, or sympathize with him.
- Trust him.
- Expect sympathy or understanding.
- Go against your better judgment.
- Compromise your values.
- Believe that he really is too good to be true.
- Think he will treat you differently than he does others.
- Be taken in by the bad-boy behavior.
- Think you are getting something.
- Think he respects you.
- Share about yourself.
- Confide secrets (hopes, plans, dreams, and fantasies).
- Become enamored of his power/personality/charm/charisma.
- Be seduced (by money, power, sex, deals, lifestyle, prestige, revenge, ego, flattery, or social, political, or philosophical issues).
- Become partners.
- Try to manipulate back.
- Try to con.
- Send for therapy (individual or group).
- Believe that if it is written (e.g., a contract), he feels bound to honor it.
- Appear weak.
- Lie for him.
- Think a confrontation will change things.
- Expect him to take responsibility.

Remember ——————————————————————————————

If it doesn't work, don't keep doing it!

——————————————————————————————————

How to Deal with ASPDs
What You Can Do
(Do these mainly to keep your perspective.)

- Be wary.
- Mistrust.
- Be indifferent.
- Have facts to support you.
- Question everything.
- Be entertained.
- Say no.
- Give nothing.
- Confront (although it will go nowhere, it will keep you on track).
- Be cautious when you begin to lie to yourself.
- Remember that you will be blackmailed if you do something wrong.
- Run from mental and physical abuse.
- Avoid guilt.
- When unsure, talk with others who you know are solid.
- Point out his behavior to others.
- Call him on his behavior and levy consequences.
- Stand your ground.
- Trust your feelings.

Remember ——————————————————————————————

*If you do the above, the ASPD's behavior will worsen. He will try to charm
and entice you more or threaten.*

——————————————————————————————————

TYPICAL CONVERSATION: REVISED
(AFTER DR. BOB READ THIS CHAPTER)

Dr. Bob, a psychiatrist, rushes to return Clyde's urgent phone call when
he finds a moment. Clyde had seen Dr. Bob for only one appointment many

months ago, during which Clyde requested some pain medication for recurring migraines. Clyde did not make a return appointment, nor follow up with Dr. Bob for some blood tests ordered. Clyde, having given wrong insurance information, never paid his bill. Before making the phone call, Dr. Bob reviewed Clyde's chart and carefully noted this information to himself.

Dr. Bob: "Hi, Clyde. What can I do for you?"

Clyde: "Hello, Dr. Bob. I really appreciate your taking the time to give me a call back. Are you still dressing so well? I remember that fabulous suit you were wearing."

Dr. Bob: "Thank you. Clyde, why did you call? It's been many months since you were here."

Clyde: "When I was last in to see you, I was very impressed with how much you seemed to care about your patients. You appeared genuinely concerned about their suffering and how you might help them. I felt exceptionally good when I left your office."

Dr. Bob: "Yes?"

Clyde: "I knew you were the person I could rely on. I have had some personal problems within my family and also have been involved in some stressful business dealings. As a result, my migraines have returned. I need a prescription for something stronger than you last ordered. Perhaps something with a narcotic base in it like other doctors have given me in the past. Your secretary said that I would have to come in to see you, but, and I know you'll understand this with your busy schedule, my time is very tight right now . . . and the pain is excruciating. Dr. Bob, I know you have your rules about this sort of thing, but could you make an exception and please call in a prescription? I'll be happy to make a future appointment when my schedule opens up. I know I still owe some money. I tried going for those lab tests, but the place was always closed when I went over. I'll try again tomorrow. My pain is taking away that quality time I spend with my family, and it is affecting my wife and my children, as well as business."

Dr. Bob: "I note here in your chart that after you didn't show up for two appointments and didn't call to cancel; we sent you a termination letter. I see it was sent certified/return receipt, and you did get it. We also haven't received any payment on your outstanding balance. I'm sorry, Clyde, but you are no longer my patient, and I can't prescribe any medication."

Clyde: "I quite understand your feelings about this. I was traveling for several weeks. I'll bet my wife signed for the letter and never showed it to me. I told my secretary to cancel those appointments with you since I'd be out of town. You're in business, so you know what getting good help is like. I would consider it a personal favor if you would call in a prescription. I'll make an appointment right now and guarantee you I'll be there."

Dr. Bob: "I'm sorry, Clyde, but I chose to terminate our relationship because of your unreliability. I believe that that really hasn't changed."

Clyde: "Well, the medical society will be hearing about your unethical practices and your lack of sympathy to someone in need. I thought I could trust you."

Dr. Bob: "I regret that you feel that way. Goodbye."

THE TYPES OF PEOPLE WHO ARE MOST TRAPPED IN RELATIONSHIPS WITH ASPDS

Most of us are usually trusting and open, which means that most of us have been duped by an ASPD sometime in our lives. People who are easily taken and swayed by others, including the insecure, the abused, the guilty, and the giving are fast victims for ASPDs. If you are easily led or have suffered abuse, the ASPD will exploit you. If you have some wish, fantasy, or desire (and who doesn't?), ASPDs will use it to control. If the ASPD is in a fix, he appeals to the rescuer for help and promises something to the rescuer to suck him or her in.

Those who find themselves attracted to the bravado, the fast life, or the worldly ways of the ASPD are also easily duped and used. ASPDs particularly like individuals who think they are with it and pretty slick themselves. In these situations, the ASPD plays into that false confidence and excels in his manipulations.

Remember ——————————————————————————————————

It is about power, money, or sex.

Remember ——————————————————————————————

If it doesn't work, don't keep doing it!

———————————————————————————————————————

SUMMARY

ASPDs are the con men of the world. They lure us in with promises of fulfillment but wind up controlling us. They lie. They cheat. They have regard only for rules that serve them. Their promises compromise your values, which is how you become trapped.

CHAPTER 5

Intense, Demanding, Extreme, and Definitely Unstable: The Borderline Personality Disorder (BPD)

Think *Fatal Attraction*

"I hate you. Don't leave me."

Some years ago, a movie called *Fatal Attraction* appeared in theaters. Most people (especially the men) came away from the movie impressed by the extreme consequences that a one-night stand could have. The plot develops from the married male lead having a sexual encounter with an extremely attractive, intense, and mysterious woman. Although the tryst was for only the one night as far as the man was concerned, the woman did not see it that way. In the short time that she was with the man (and without any commitments from him), the woman had convinced herself that he was her *ideal* man, the ultimate concerned and caring lover who would bring her true happiness. When she found that he did not share the same conclusion, her rage at feeling abandoned eventually proved fatal for someone. This movie brilliantly portrays the forceful and extreme behavior of a person with borderline personality disorder (BPD) as we all might encounter it in our everyday lives.

Whether you are a man or a woman, the BPD can trap you with the profound intensity of her or his personality. Deep passion pervades a BPD's behaviors and can be quite ensnaring. Often, the seductive quality comes from a profound inner need and seeming vulnerability that can, initially, have its own ineluctable quality. The border on which the BPD functions is the edge between sanity and madness. BPDs' perception of the world is so fragile that frequently they interpret others' behaviors in a way so skewed from what is actually happening that you would consider the BPD psychotic. BPDs control you with intense emotion and behavioral extremes that initially can appear quite captivating. As you unwittingly become more involved with these individuals, there may appear to be no way to exit.

Often, when the BPD is a family member, you experience frustrating years of trying to reason with the BPD and find that you have made no progress. The BPD can bring a family into turmoil with accusations and paranoia, and by turning one person against the other. BPDs have the ability to bring your life into a type of chaos you could not imagine. For example, they manipulate others with one of their recurring behaviors, self-mutilation (cutting themselves), which has won them the description of being "slicers and dicers."

Red-Flag Feelings in You

Strong attraction to her profound intensity (her sexuality, mystery, neediness, despair, or emptiness)
Confusion in the chaos of the relationship
Fear of his extremes
Anger or guilt

A BPD will manipulate and control you with the extreme intensity of his or her passion (especially rage and emptiness) in whatever area you become involved. As a health professional, you want to help; in business, you may be part of an intense power struggle; personally, you could be overpowered in a chaotic relationship that she will not let go of ("She might kill herself if I leave") or one in which you may feel compelled to help this tortured (and torturing) soul. Because people with BPD are predominantly women, I use female pronouns in the remainder of this chapter to refer to individuals with borderline personality disorder.

Picture This

Who Are the BPDs You Might See?

This person *seethes* with anger if you are late for a date.

This micromanager constantly looks over your shoulder, fearing that you are doing something against her.

This fun date believes you are going to marry her after one good time together.

This client demands your time to the allotted minute and fumes if you stop too soon.

This woman idealizes you as perfect one day and then degrades you as vermin the next, without any overt reason.

This person splits people who usually work well together into opposing factions.

Despite your proven trustworthiness, this person believes you will abandon her at any moment because she is so evil or because you are deceitful.

This person believes that if you do not totally agree with her, you hate her.

Picture This

Professional Life

Because of the immensity of the therapeutic demands that BPDs make, many mental health professionals have deliberately chosen not to engage them in treatment, which should tip you off about the difficulty involved in dealing with BPDs. A person with BPD will present herself to you with such an extreme need for help that you will feel wretched if you do not lend a hand. As you try to help, you find yourself in a situation where more intense and unrealistic demands are repeatedly made on you—demands that the BPD fully expects you to meet.

If you are seeing a BPD in a professional context—as, for example, a counselor or a psychiatrist—you could expect the following types of behavior and circumstances:

This person repeatedly calls you in the middle of the night to leave drunken messages that you have failed her, even though you may have only consulted with her once.

A seventeen-year-old girl's parents bring her to the hospital. She has multiple crisscrosses of superficial lacerations going up and down both arms. She is dressed in black. She admits in a casual manner having had sex with three guys the night before "to get even with my girlfriends." One of the guys was fourteen years old.

Your client refuses to leave your office, or may even stalk you in a belief that you owe her something. She has already sent you, her therapist, a mutilated doll as a baby gift when you cut back your hours to care for your newborn.

You have just met this individual, who now believes that *she* is the center of your life. She thinks that you are perfect and that you want to be with her . . . always.

This person comes to your office and conveys to you such a profound sense of need (her anguish and despair) that you feel powerless in refusing to help her.

You listen to a message on your answering machine that a person is about to kill herself, which is your fault for not answering the phone.

Your client breaks glass into pieces and then inserts the shards into various parts of her body—her arms, legs, breasts, and so on.

Early in your appointment with her, the BPD will tell you about:

• The profound unhappiness in her life.
• The evil people and things that have caused this.
• Her abandonment by an uncaring world.
• Her rage, her despair, her emptiness.
• Her confusion.
• Her past extreme behaviors or fantasies (drinking, drugging, suicide attempts, self-mutilation, sexual extremes).

Initially, she may be seductive in her behavior, but usually in a professional situation, she will dwell on the above types of actions. The BPD has a very tenuous sense of who she is. She has a void where her self should be, and relies on seeing her self-worth expressed in how you treat her. Unlike the histrionic personality disorder (HPD), who sees the attention she generates as a sign of her worth as a person but who can flexibly drift from one to another seeking to be noticed, the BPD is more rigid in how she reacts to others and has a much more fragile ego. The BPD is very concrete in how she views the world: it is black or white. The BPD has an exquisite sensitivity to acceptance and rejection. From the moment she walks into your office, the BPD believes that you literally either love her or hate her. In each minute of your appointment(s) with her, she is carefully assessing how you treat her. Each time you see her, the BPD views each of your acts as expressive of your feelings for her. The BPD is incapable of developing any bond of trust or consistency with you as you interact. For example, if you are late one time in meeting with her, all else is forgotten and the BPD believes you have turned against her.

If you are a health-care professional, you are liable to become involved with the extremes of the BPD because of your position as a caregiver—although anyone who renders help, guidance, or advice in a professional capacity is at risk. The BPD initially idealizes any caregiver as being all-kind, all-giving, and all-accepting. If this fragile ideal is disturbed as she watches your behavior, you become not only a disappointment to her, but also a hateful and evil person. She may become vengeful toward you, depending on the hurt the BPD imagines you have inflicted on her.

Remember

BPDs function in a world of extremes. They have an exquisite sensitivity to perceived abandonment. They may even see your most innocent gesture as an instance of wronging, and the response could be rage. BPDs often feel abandoned, yet drive others away with their rage.

True Life

True-Life Adventure 1:
Raging Rhonda and Dr. Bob

From outward appearances, Rhonda was a successful, well-functioning young woman in her midthirties. She had an MBA from an Ivy-league school and held a responsible job at an insurance company. Rhonda made an appointment with Dr. Bob, a psychiatrist, to discuss her chronic depression and loneliness. Upon meeting her in his office, Dr. Bob was impressed by the drabness that Rhonda conveyed—in her clothing, her looks, her description of her house, and her job. Dr. Bob, at first, attributed this to Rhonda's chronic depression and negativism.

Rhonda had no friends. She did not date and, in fact, had had few dates her whole life. Her life followed a regimented track, from intense study in high school to the demands of business school and then the MBA program, with a structure that continued into her present job. Rhonda described her teenage years as filled with apprehensions and insecurities far beyond those of normal teens. She had gone through a cycle in her teens of cutting herself on her upper legs (so no one would see) "to relieve the pain."

Rhonda was always very wary of others and saw them as hurtful to her. As a result, she stayed at a cautious distance, and consequently led a very lonely life. Dr. Bob tried both medication and psychotherapy in hopes of helping Rhonda with the emptiness she felt. She responded to neither. Rhonda would frequently complain about coworkers whom she perceived were out to get her and bosses who treated her badly and did not appreciate the work she did.

Dr. Bob recurrently tried unsuccessfully to help Rhonda deal with her seeing the entire world as extremely unfriendly to her, including the grocery checkout person who deliberately took too long, the bank teller who did not smile at her, or a repairman who could not give an exact time of his coming. All of these things Rhonda took as specifically designed to hurt her. Rhonda trusted no one. In her, Dr. Bob sensed a tremendous loneliness and despair.

Rhonda cycled from feeling quite superior to everyone to feeling very inadequate and extremely sensitive to any form of what she thought was disapproval. She looked to others to confirm that she was a good person. However, at the slightest hint of something negative (such as someone not smiling at her), she felt the confirmation of her worst fears—that she was bad. There was no in-between with Rhonda: If you did not agree with her, you were against her. Since most of us do not live up to others' expectations all of the time, Rhonda went around with a constant deep rage within her.

Her fury took the form of paranoia at times, with Rhonda convinced that everyone (most of whom were probably indifferent to her) were deliberately out to hurt her in some way. Dr. Bob discussed with Rhonda her need to be loved and her fear of abandonment. However, with each therapy meeting Rhonda remembered nothing about their previous discussions on how she distorts her view of others based on her own emotions. Each appointment found Rhonda seething about some new wrong done to her.

It became clear to Dr. Bob that Rhonda's wrath pervaded her life and that anyone who might get to know Rhonda would likely reject her since she acted in unlikeable ways. Dr. Bob tried to be consistent and nonjudgmental, but when he confronted Rhonda with her misguided and distorted anger, he also fell into Rhonda's bin of rejecting humanity. She became furious with him if he started an appointment a minute or two late, or if he stopped the appointment even thirty seconds before the allotted time. She saw this as a sign of his not wanting to spend time with her, which may have been true.

With an air of entitlement, Rhonda screamed for longer appointments, making Dr. Bob worry that he would only make her more furious if he did not give in to her demands. She attacked his integrity as a doctor and threatened lawsuits. After one angry session, Dr. Bob became concerned that Rhonda might become physically assaultive. Dr. Bob was perplexed.

On the one hand, Rhonda was critical of everything about him while on the other, she wanted more time with him. Dr. Bob saw himself going from being a professional who had become very involved in trying to help Rhonda to someone fast becoming defensive and self-protective.

As raging Rhonda walked out of what became their last appointment together, she contemptuously ran her arm along Dr. Bob's desk and knocked to the floor everything on it. She did the same thing to his secretary's desk. Preparing for the worst, Dr. Bob had already discussed such behavior with Rhonda as unacceptable and grounds for terminating treatment, which he finally did. But it did not end there.

Rhonda began to stalk Dr. Bob. She would wait in his parking lot until the end of office hours and try to follow him to find out where he lived. She took pictures of him as he drove by her. She spilled paint remover all over his car; she put dirt into his gas tank. Rhoda phoned Dr. Bob and said, "You told me I was very sensitive to being abandoned, and here you are doing just that to me. How can you call yourself a professional, you bastard! I think you just wanted to have sex with me. You played me. Now you're really screwing me."

Finally, Dr. Bob went to the police after a large envelope came to his home marked "Gift." Dr. Bob's six-year-old was delighted to open the surprise package with no one knowing what was inside. What they found was the severed head of a rat. Although there was no return address, Dr. Bob knew who had sent it.

Remember

BPDs can initially appear higher functioning, but they have a very tenuous grasp of reality. As a professional, you will be very challenged to maintain a consistent, reliable, helpful role while at the same time avoiding the BPD's tendency to include you in her paranoia.

True Life

True-Life Adventure 2:
Maiming Martha and Attorney Goodfellow

Martha fell in love with her lawyer, Attorney Goodfellow. He was simply a nice man with a warm personality doing his job helping her with a legal problem. But very quickly Martha took this as their having a "special" relationship. Martha found she could not tolerate Attorney Goodfellow "seeing" other women, that is, his other female clients. Martha would sit in the parking lot and watch the women entering and exiting his office. As she felt increasingly jealous and betrayed, Martha would sit in her car and cut her arm with a razor.

This behavior escalated to where Martha, when at home and brooding on Attorney Goodfellow's "relationships" with other women, would choose between either cutting herself or placing her arm in near-boiling water. For Martha, this act "relieved the pain."

Remember

Since you stand for some expertise that BPDs may see as particularly desirous, their expectations of you as the professional can be extreme. They can be erratic, impulsive, intensely moody, and condemning way beyond the scope of the professional relationship. Their extreme distortion of reality hallmarks BPDs. They have no normal ways of calming themselves, and they escape into impulsive sex, drugs, alcohol, food, and/or self-mutilation as ways of relieving tension.

True Life

True-Life Adventure 3:
Ephemeral Emogene and Ms. Martin, Vocational Counselor

Emogene is a third-year college student who has sought help from Ms. Martin on several occasions, usually at the beginning of each year, and then midway through. Recurrently, Emogene seeks out Ms. Martin's help after she once again finds her heart's desire in terms of a major course of study and what she wants to do with her life. Emogene flits from one major to another as she identifies different professors who become her ideal and on whom she wants to pattern her life.

Ms. Martin: "Well, Emogene, here you again wanting to change majors. This will be the seventh time. What is it this time?"

Emogene: "I went on a dig with Professor Jones last summer and fell in love with archaeology . . . and him. This is what I want to do."

Ms. Martin: "You said that before about English drama and Professor Howell. When you found out that he was married, you dropped the course and tried to kill yourself. That was not a good time for you. I hate to ask, but did you have any sexual dealings with Professor Jones?"

Emogene: "Howell turned out to be a complete bastard. He knew how much I cared about him and drama, and yet he still treated me with indifference. And, yes, I did have an affair with Professor Jones over the summer. I came to know him like no one has ever known him. I am certain I can answer his every need. He loves everything about me."

Ms. Martin: "Isn't this a little extreme? Each time we talk, I get the impression that you choose an area of concentration based on how one teacher or another feels about the subject rather than what you really want.

You seem to live vicariously through them and their lives. You can't think that just because someone else is happy in what they're doing, you will be too. You'll only keep getting disappointed over and over again. "

Emogene: "So? What's wrong with that? What's wrong with loving the same things as someone else? Why do you always have to put me down? If you don't want to help, just say so."

Remember

The BPD has no sense of who she is as a person. She looks entirely to others for total fulfillment, care, and direction, while at the same time the relationships are chaotic and intense since BPDs always see others as letting them down. Constantly changing goals, jobs, and relationships pervade the BPD's life. As a professional, you will also fail her.

True Life

True-Life Adventure 4:
Willing Wanda and Guileless Glenn, Social Worker

Wanda sought out Glenn's counseling for her problems with relationships with men. Brenda told Glenn that she tried to be a pleasant and sociable person and was concerned that she was too compliant and giving with others. Brenda worried that these reasons explained why many men did not continue to call her.

Glenn was a caring fellow and immediately conveyed his desire to help. In their first appointment, Glenn was personable yet professional. He asked many questions and inspired Wanda. With their next appointment, Wanda revealed that she, in response to Glenn's clear and special concern for her, had fallen in love with him. She said that she felt that his treating her in such a special way suggested his strong feelings for her. Glenn was surprised and became quite concerned with himself as he wondered how he could have given off such signals.

Remember

BPDs are so needy and lost that they misinterpret your behavior. If you are nice, BPDs infer that you love them. The other extreme is also true: If you are not nice, you must hate them.

True Life

True-Life Adventure 5:
Furious Phoebe and Counselor Karen

Phoebe scheduled an appointment with Karen as stipulated by the court for anger management. Phoebe had been arrested for disorderly conduct.

Phoebe admits that she has severe mood swings and rages, but she blames them primarily on her husband Jake. In Phoebe's opinion, it is all Jake's fault for letting her down by not making her happy as he promised.

"When we were dating, Jake promised me that our lives would always be happy and filled with sunshine. Well, he lied," Phoebe tells Karen. Karen knows that it can be an adjustment as the romance of early marriage begins to wear off and day-to-day reality intrudes. She tries to help Phoebe see this.

Karen: "You told me Jake is kind to you, loves you, earns a good living, and does many things to help around the house. I know it's not always sunshine and roses, but he seems to be a good husband."

Phoebe: "Yes, he is, but I'm not happy all of the time like he said I would be. And when I get depressed, he's not always there for me. I call him at work, but sometimes he can't talk or maybe he just doesn't want to talk to me."

Karen begins to see that Phoebe has no desire to see another perspective about life. Phoebe goes on to tell Karen many intimate details of her life, including her past drug use, her being arrested for shoplifting, and her promiscuity.

"It wasn't so much the sex. It was that just being held by someone made me feel desirable," Phoebe tells Karen. She also describes her present fear that she might be gay and her recently picking up guys at a local bar "just to see if I was still attractive."

Phoebe sees Karen for more appointments and begins to request "special" times (longer and more frequent appointments). Phoebe then accuses Karen: "You haven't helped me. I'm still unhappy. I come in here and spill my soul.

You say a few things that I guess you think are important, but I don't feel any better. "

Karen, thinking that Phoebe's comment now allows her to make a great point, says, "I guess you thought I was going to make you happy just like you said Jake promised. I guess that I also have let you down." Karen hopes that Phoebe will now see that she herself has the unrealistic expectations of people that bring about her own unhappiness.

However, Phoebe yells, "You got that right. You can bet I'll be telling anyone I can about what a lying bitch you are. You take my money and probably laugh when I leave. Like it's my fault that I believe people and they let me down. I came here to get help with my anger, and you only make it worse. The world sucks . . . and so do you."

Remember

Because BPDs think in a paranoid way, they cannot recognize their own complicity in their unhappiness. They perceive authority figures often in an idealized way at first, but their rage quickly surfaces.

Picture This

Business Life

Since they can cause such havoc, BPDs generally do not hold employment positions long. However, some BPDs can suppress their paranoia and keep their seething outside of work. Then they may hold a position for a long period of time depending on how much stress comes with the job. More often, BPDs will be independent (consulting) or have their own businesses where they might use their pathology to make money, like owning a security firm, where they can turn paranoia into profit. Venues such as the media, retail, show business, music, or other extremely competitive areas may tolerate the extremes of the BPD. Certainly, a business operation with a philosophy of distrust, hypervigilance, domination, and revenge would welcome a BPD.

In the working world, BPDs might manifest themselves as:

• The manager or coworker who is constantly in your face about your work and how you spend your time.

• The character on your team who appears, at first, to have some definite and focused opinions. However, there is no room for discussion. She splits the team into rival factions rather than keeping the focus on the project goal.

• The person whose mood is unpredictable or can be changed by the slightest occurrence, and the bad mood is not mild; it can be raging.

• The individual who micromanages out of fears that you will steal, undermine, and/or leave her at any moment, despite no such indications on your part.

• The employee who will make statements totally out in left field.

• The person who is constantly changing things on impulse.

• The person who becomes furious beyond understanding if you are late, as though you have betrayed her.

True Life

True-Life Adventure 1:
Black Betty, M.D., and Dr. Bob

Dr. Bob, a psychiatrist, had just been appointed the medical director of a hospital and clinic when he learned that Dr. Betty had been already hired from out of state and was due to join the staff soon. Dr. Betty had worked for the hospital several years prior, and some of the old-timers remembered her vaguely and not too fondly. Although a starting date was reached, Dr. Betty phoned a few times to change it since she, a single mother, could not arrange things for her children and had to have things perfect for their move.

When they finally met, Dr. Bob could not get over her appearance. Dr. Betty dressed completely in black, wore no makeup, and seemed to be try- ing for a pallid and ghostly look. He smiled to himself and thought of her as Black Betty. *But she's a professional,* he thought, and did not think any fur- ther about it. Early into the job, Dr. Bob stopped by Dr. Betty's office to see how things were going. The office had an eerie quality about it. It was dark with only one small lamp and a lit candle for illumination. Dr. Betty was dressed all in black.

"I want to make my office comfortable for my patients," Dr. Betty responded when asked about the ambience. "Please sit over here in the most comfortable chair. You must have so much stress in your job. I've looked forward to working with you. I am really a team player and want to learn all I can under your leadership," she whispered. Dr. Bob was, instead, becoming increasingly uncomfortable with the conversation and wondered if Dr. Betty was behaving a bit seductively with him, her new boss.

As she went on to describe her new colleagues in the department, Dr. Betty moved her chair closer and told Dr. Bob how she had concerns about their practice of medicine and how this might put the hospital into some dangerous liability issues. Dr. Bob had worked with these other doctors and had never noted such problems.

As days passed, Dr. Betty was quickly transferred from seeing patients admitted to the hospital because she caused such friction between the nurses, patients, and other doctors with her almost libelous accusations against the staff. She was clever in splitting the different groups against each other. She could be quite sarcastic, with frequent verbal outbursts. Shortly after her transfer to treating only outpatients, the same problems reoccurred.

Dr. Bob was not a confrontational type of person. When he reassigned Dr. Betty, he did so with words to her that he was looking for the best place for her to fit in. As the conflicts continued with Dr. Betty undermining staff ideas and plans for treatment, and her threatening to call various government agencies because of her concerns at the clinic, Dr. Bob had to be more direct.

"What are your concerns with patient care?" he asked.

Dr. Betty replied by listing some vague and poorly defined issues. When Dr. Bob dismissed them as having no real basis, Dr. Betty replied, "Well, I guess you, too, don't mind breaking the law. I'm embarrassed for you and for your staff."

Thus ended Dr. Bob's being held in high esteem by Dr. Betty as a role model and fearless leader. He now was the evil-handed person working against her, this outstanding team player. As far as Dr. Betty was concerned, everyone had let her down and all had turned against her.

Dr. Betty then requested a three-month leave of absence because of vague physical problems brought on by the stress of work. When this request was denied, Dr. Betty, dressed in black, resigned.

Afterward, she made good on her threats of reporting the hospital with several local, state, and federal regulatory groups. She subsequently held three more jobs in the area, each of them lasting about three months.

Remember

If you do not agree with a BPD, you are against her.

True Life

True-Life Adventure 2:
Nasty Nadia and Good-Guy Matt

Matt came to work for Nadia because his previous corporate job was becoming increasingly stressful and demanding. He had asked around about his new employer before taking the job and found out that Nadia had a history of being difficult to work with. Matt was in the mood to work for a small business rather than a big corporation. He felt that nothing could be as bad as his previous employment. Matt was wrong. The job was in a very competitive marketing area of the music business. One person undercutting another, stealing clients, and lying about the competitors was commonplace. Matt was very bright and self-motivated, and he had initiative and integrity. Once he understood a job, he would take charge and need little direction. In Nadia's mind, these qualities were not admirable.

Nadia was in her late forties. She was a former cocaine addict who lived alone after her divorce. Nadia had her office set up so she could closely watch all of her employees as they went through the business day. She did this because she felt she needed to guard constantly against her employees somehow talking advantage of her. She vigilantly made sure that they did not talk on the phone for nonbusiness matters, do private e-mailing, pilfer information to sell to other companies, or simply steal paper clips. Nadia was a paranoid micromanager. In her world, Matt's initiative and take-charge approach threatened her and her sense of control.

Nadia was prone to unexplained temper tantrums and mood swings. She might sit in her office for hours just watching people and then attack with some inappropriate criticism. If confronted by some daring employee about her unfair comments, Nadia would never explain where she was coming from or apologize. She would spend long periods in her office brooding. If the employees were silent after one of her harangues, Nadia sometimes would try to be nice, but this tack was usually very short-lived.

Nadia would rant to her female employees, in front of Matt, about how low men are, what cheats and liars they were. Matt would try to discuss with Nadia how badly her behavior affected him and the other staff members. She countered with statements that had nothing to do with Matt's point and then walked away in a huff. If he wanted vacation time, Matt would be obliged to ask for it many weeks ahead. Nadia would then make him feel guilty that he wanted his deserved time off, as though he were sucking the life out of her.

If traffic were exceptionally bad and he was a bit late, Nadia would grill him with many questions about his route and what time he left, and then state that she felt he was doing it on purpose.

"Don't you like it here?" she would ask him, with Matt holding in his true answer.

She would repeatedly go over office procedures as though he were a new employee. Matt found he never gained any trust from Nadia about the job he did. He felt guilty about not pleasing his boss, while frustrated in the fact that whatever he did, he knew he could not satisfy her. Like all good guys, Matt tried to work things out. He eventually left for a healthier place to work.

Remember ———————————————————————

The BPD's paranoia and suspiciousness can be so confusing (since it is so crazy) that you become immobilized in always defending yourself and trying to make things right.

True Life

True-Life Adventure 3:
Fanatical Frieda and the Cause

Frieda, a longtime activist and crusader for justice, obtained a job with a human rights organization that had high social goals. To Frieda, the objectives of the organization were less important than the notion that she would have something to which she could attach her passion. She imagined herself becoming an outspoken supporter, a zealot for the cause. In a short time, Frieda became the righteous avenger aggressively pursuing converts to the cause and a strong promoter of its basic goals. As she became more outspoken, Frieda's venom and vehemence began to frighten others, with her being asked to tone down her attitude.

As a result, Frieda was crestfallen and felt betrayed by the organization for which she believed she would have died. After a vicious argument with her director, Frieda left to find another cause.

Remember —————————————————————————

BPDs often seek people or groups as reinforcements for their distorted views and as vehicles to allow them to vent their fury. There certainly are extreme groups where this may occur, but BPDs generally find no space in more conventional organizations.

True Life

True-Life Adventure 4:
Mischievous Marge in the Business World

Marge was extremely bright and had an expertise that was highly sought after in business. She acquired a well-paying job right out of college. Since her first months focused on her learning the job, she was in a fairly structured situation with her boss overseeing much of her work. Marge welcomed his guidance and felt secure with his support. She enjoyed their frequent meetings and his encouragement. Marge was viewed as an excellent worker who was always to work on time and responsible in getting her work projects done, although she seemed to be somewhat of a loner. She responded well to praise, but when minor criticisms were mentioned (expected with a new job), Marge would not report to work the next day.

Two things occurred that did Marge in. First, Marge's boss became less directive and involved with her. He saw Marge as fitting well into her work. Since he was not a micromanager, he tried to give her more space in which to grow. However, Marge saw this as his being more aloof and distant. She obsessed over how she must have displeased him, but she dwelt more on what she believed was his abandoning her to let her fail. When she confronted her boss about this, he was puzzled and began to explain his aims. Being a BPD, Marge did not have the capacity to accept this and thought that he was lying to her. Behind her boss's back, she went to her coworkers and tried to turn them against this "nasty" man.

Then her boss recommended her for a promotion that he thought she deserved. Marge fell apart. She accused her boss of wanting to hurt her career and herself personally by rejecting her. She carried on about how hard she had worked, but now she felt that she was being cast aside, like a bad employee being punished. Marge resigned from her position in a rage about how badly she had been treated.

Remember ————————————————————————

No matter how capable BPDs may appear, they are very dependent. They strongly rely on structure from others to rule their lives. Having less direction makes them confused and feel far adrift. If let go, even to a promotion or more responsibility within the job, BPDs see it as abandonment and become overwhelmed since they must rely more on themselves.

Picture This

Personal Life

In the beginning of a personal relationship, BPDs may appear alluring, enticing, independent, assertive, and very willing to please; alternatively, they may appear needy, alone, or adrift. How they impress you will depend on how BPDs perceive you and what they feel they have to do to get your interest.

However, the BPD's ragings, sarcasm, bitterness, mistrust, and extreme behaviors—like self-mutilation (for example, cutting or burning herself), suicide attempts, or stalking—can definitely take the dazzle out of a relationship. Some people early on recognize that continuing to see a BPD is something undesirable and will walk away before they become further entrenched. Many others become ensnared in a relationship out of confusion, guilt, passivity, or the foolish belief that they might help this person.

The families of BPDs (parents, siblings, and spouses who did not get away soon enough) cannot walk away so easily and bear a profound burden in trying to maintain any semblance of a relationship with this difficult personality. In your personal life, you might find the BPD to be:

- The woman who seems to read your mind and know your fantasies. She can be anything you want her to be.
- The person who is coy and challenging.
- The stalker.
- The woman whose moods flare from one extreme to the other in an instant.
- The person full of fury at you for insignificant reasons.

True Life

True-Life Adventure 1:
Evil Elsa and Her Family, the Woefuls

Mr. and Mrs. Woeful sought advice and information from Dr. Nick about their daughter Elsa, who was causing emotional chaos in the family, which included Mom, Dad, Elsa, Elsa's brother and sister, and Elsa's husband, Dirk.

Her parents, soft-spoken and kindly, told Dr. Nick that Elsa had always seemed a difficult child throughout her life. Mrs. Woeful said, "She was always a hard person to love. When she was young, if I tried to hug her, she would push me away. If I walked away, she would cry because I wasn't hugging her. As we raised her, there was always some kind of conflict going on.

From our other two kids, we had a taste of teenage rebellion, but Elsa went way beyond that."

Mr. Woeful added, "Everything was an argument, a power struggle. Elsa didn't know when to give in. She turned every little argument into something her life depended on. She could not just leave an issue. We know a teenager will say 'I hate you' to a parent when she doesn't get her way, but when Elsa said it, I could really feel the venom behind it."

During high school, Elsa became involved in drugs and indiscriminate sex. "There was no possibility of an even semirational discussion with her," Mrs. Woeful went on. "She was always in one form of trouble or another, so it was difficult to praise her. God knows we tried. When we attempted to discuss her behavior, she would quickly become furious with us for attacking her. As much as we tried to understand, she saw us as either totally with her or totally against her; there was no middle ground. In her mind, we hated her, and that was that. I am embarrassed to admit that there were times when I did have very hateful feelings toward her."

Elsa eventually graduated from high school and went to college, but she dropped out after the second year. She did not return home and wrote that she was going to travel around and see the country. For two years the Woefuls would hear from her sporadically. Then Elsa showed up in a nearby town. She was married to Dirk and pregnant. The Woefuls were happy to see their daughter again, but, as in so many times in the past, it was not under the best circumstance. They wanted to be supportive but also wanted to share their concerns. Elsa had not changed. Even the simplest questions were met with anger that her "vicious" parents were condemning her.

What drove the Woefuls to consult with Dr. Nick was the latest and worst development. Elsa had accused Mr. Woeful, her father, of sexually molesting her as a child. She said this knowledge came to her after watching a TV program about repressed memories. Mr. Woeful adamantly denied this, with his wife also supporting him as to how incredible a charge this was.

Elsa had also told her sister and brother about her memory and was so convincing that she now had the family split, with her sister believing her and her brother incensed over the accusation. Elsa tried to get her sister to admit that their father molested her, but her sister denied any such experiences while growing up. Elsa, whose child was now two years old, was refusing to see her parents ever again (Dad for obvious reasons and Mom because she sided with Dad), as well as not letting her parents see their first grandson. Mrs. Woeful was heartbroken about not being able to see the little boy. Elsa's husband, having experienced Elsa's extremes, had initially been sympathetic to the Woefuls and met with them secretly so they could see their grandson. However, Elsa found out about it and caused such a problem at home that the meetings stopped.

Mr. and Mrs. Woeful were hoping that Dr. Nick could give them some insight into how they might reconcile with their daughter. Could the family be reconciled? Would Elsa relent? Would this family find true happiness? Unlikely. And that was the sad news that Dr. Nick conveyed to Mr. and Mrs. Woeful.

Remember

There is no reasoning with BPDs. You can try, but you will continue to be miserable in the process. If you have to stay in the relationship (like in a family), you must keep a distance from the BPD in order to be able to tolerate the situation. If you have the choice, run.

True Life

True-Life Adventure 2:
Loose Leslie and Ken

Ken, a doctor, married Leslie for her beauty and intelligence. Ken was also initially taken with Leslie's doting on him and her seeming to be able to read his mind about whatever he wanted. *Leslie is too good to be true,* Ken thought. Although gifted, Leslie was never quite able to find a job that suited her. Since her husband could afford it, she decided to stay at home. She could be found about the town at the club for lunch, at the fitness center with her personal trainer, and out shopping. Leslie increasingly took Ken for granted and would daily argue with him about his not fulfilling her.

Ken was committed to his marriage and to having a family. He became very upset when Leslie informed him that she had decided against having children. Ken's anger worsened when he learned that Leslie was sleeping with a number of men in town, including her personal trainer, the guy who cleaned her windows, the car salesman who sold her the new BMW, and the cop who had not given her the last speeding ticket. When Ken confronted Leslie, she attacked him with a pair of scissors. After this episode, Ken would come home to find rooms in a mess with Leslie having broken vases, lamps, mirrors, and windows. On one occasion, Ken arrived home to find his clothes slashed and lying in pieces about his closet. He noticed his pants were slashed only in the crotch area. Leslie would call his office many times in the day and frequently threaten suicide or rant drunkenly to his secretary. When Ken would try to have a discussion with her, Leslie refused and became hysterical. She rejected marital counseling, saying that Ken would turn any therapist against her. Her own four attempts at therapy ended with Leslie feeling the advice given was worthless since it focused on her responsibility for her own behavior.

In Leslie's mind, the marriage's troubles were Ken's fault. Ken, she believed, was driving her to her extreme behaviors. Ken became increasingly fearful when they argued and knew he had to remain calm when Leslie's insults became so severe. Leslie would taunt Ken to hit her. When he did not, Leslie would scratch herself and then call the police alleging that Ken had attacked her.

The divorce was bloody. Leslie accused Ken of sadistic sex and hinted that he was sexually attracted to children. She maintained that this was the reason why she did not want children, as she feared her husband would molest them. As the divorce progressed, Leslie would send Ken sexually explicit e-mails, some with pictures of her and other men. She spent increasing amounts of money and continued to be seen in public with other guys. Leslie fired three lawyers in the process, with the last one speeding the divorce through as quickly as possible to get rid of her.

Remember

BPDs cannot love. They are incapable of building a relationship over time as trust and confidence in the other person grows. You develop no track record of reliability or consistency with a BPD. She lives strictly according to how you are treating her at that moment. There is no working things out with a BPD. She defines how she expects to be treated, and you have no say.

True Life

True-Life Adventure 3:
Shocking Sharon and Will

Will is a successful, young business executive who meets Sharon, a consultant, at a business meeting. Sharon is intelligent, assertive, seemingly quite independent, and very attractive. Will senses a magic between them. After the meeting, Sharon lets it be known that she is unattached; Will, with his wife and children away for the week, asks her to dinner. *What could go wrong?* he asks himself.

Dinner leads to bed and fabulous sex. They part the next morning with a no-strings-attached understanding between them. Will receives a large bouquet of flowers at the office and a very suggestive card from Sharon. How can Will resist? A beautiful, sexy woman; his wife away; hot sex. They meet again.

With his wife now returning home, Will thanks Sharon for the wonderful time he has had and says goodbye. He is confident that the independent, worldly Sharon will move on. Initially when Sharon calls him at work, Will is personable and kind. He reminds Sharon that their relationship, such as it was, was fleeting and now over. Sharon does not give up so easily, with Will deciding to refuse her calls. Sharon then shows up at work and demands to speak with him. Will is bewildered and scared because Sharon now presents to him as a woman scorned and rejected rather than her previous persona of accepting the brief encounter. Sharon believes that Will is leaving his wife and children for her. Sharon begins to stalk Will. He will not go to the police since his wife may find out. She also begins to e-mail him sexual pictures filled with sadism and violence.

Late one night, Sharon calls Will at home. She tells him she is in his office, has overdosed on pills and booze, and is about to cut her wrists, and that he is to blame. Will goes to the office, finding Sharon bleeding but still alive. He calls 911, and she is taken to the hospital. Will is horrified as to how his lust has placed him in such a wretched situation.

Remember

BPDs know no boundaries, with their behaviors reaching profound extremes.

True Life

True-Life Adventure 4:
Malicious Marsha and Frank

Frank grew up in a household dominated by his mother, a critical and bitter alcoholic. Frank's father, a salesman, was frequently on the road, so Frank was left to deal with Mom, who constantly demeaned him. Frank learned to cope by turning his feelings inward and silently bore the brunt of his mother's unhappiness.

When Frank left for college, he never returned home again.

Marsha was Frank's second wife. His first marriage, which happened fresh out of college, ended quickly. He met Marsha a few years later; they married and had two children. Curiously, Frank became a salesman like his father, and Marsha took on the persona not unlike his mother: a shrewish, demanding, and always angry woman.

Frank developed an alcohol problem and for several years probably deserved Marsha's criticisms for his neglectful behavior. To his credit, Frank sobered up and changed his job so he could be home more with his family, which is when the problems really began.

Marsha would not let Frank forget his drinking and his being away. She took every opportunity to criticize him in front of their now-adult children and anyone else who might be in listening range. Marsha refused Frank any sexual relationship and insisted that he sleep in the guest room. Marsha avoided any of Frank's attempts to talk with her and to work on bettering the relationship. The more Frank tried to make things better, the more resistant Marsha became.

If they were out to dinner, Marsha would cause a scene and flee the restaurant, taking the car and leaving Frank to get home on his own. She would disappear for a weekend and become indignant if Frank asked where she went. On one of Frank's birthdays, Marsha shut the phone off so Frank would not receive any calls from his kids. She continued to lie to their children about him and swore them to secrecy saying Frank would get worse if they talked to him. His relationship with his kids became cold.

Throughout all of this, Marsha would continue to recall Frank's past drinking (despite years of sobriety) and would rage on about her suffering. Frank, passive and miserable, coped as he had learned to do many years prior—in silence.

Remember

BPDs are bitter, angry people with intense and unending resentment. You can never have a heart-to-heart talk with a BPD and walk away feeling that you have bettered the relationship. There is no intimacy with BPDs.

DISCUSSION

In psychiatry, the borderline personality disordered (BPD) individual can be the most controversial, mysterious, intriguing, yet difficult type of person to treat, and this situation certainly extends to all areas of interaction, including the professional, business, and personal spheres. Words like rage, fury, chaos, excessive, impulsive, vengeful, self-mutilating, erratic, and violent are often linked with this personality type. The BPD may at first seem very normal in first encounters and superficial interactions. But very quickly she can display not only extreme and bizarre behaviors that can be exceptionally difficult to handle, but also elicit profound frustration in dealing with her because BPDs learn nothing from working with you.

"It's like meeting a new person every day" is a common statement that applies to the BPD who sees you only in the context of that moment and how you are interacting with her. The BPD feels a profound void or emptiness inside herself. She has no sense of self and profoundly depends on you to define whether she is good or bad by how you treat her. She is like Plastic Person in her personality. She constantly tries to mold herself to fit a persona that she thinks will be pleasing to you. The BPD rapidly idealizes you in a belief that you will be that fabulous person who will always treat her well and thus indicate that she is loveable.

You build no relationship with the BPD. You are either totally accepting (meaning she is good) or you hate her (which means she is bad). Whether you were nice yesterday means nothing. Only what is happening in that moment matters to her. The BPD is exquisitely sensitive to changes, especially in a relationship. If there is anything negative, which could simply be you not being immediately there for her, she erupts not in frustration or irritation, but in rage.

Unlike the histrionic personality disordered individual who knowingly plays a role for attention, the BPD, although also looking for attention, plays no role. The BPD becomes the role she is playing. Since her 'self' is constantly changing, the BPD has no real sense of who she is.

When life does not go as she would like it to, as it has to, the BPD feels such a sense of letdown that her rage jumps forth and her mental excursion into insanity occurs. Most often, this is an excursion into paranoia. The BPD believes that if you are not totally loving and accepting, you hate her and are going to hurt her.

Some experts see BPD as a wastebasket-type of diagnosis, where all of the difficult personalities are dumped. Through the years, such names as "latent schizophrenia," "pseudoneurotic schizophrenia," the "as-if personality" (she behaves as if she is someone else), or "hysteroid person" have been applied. People with multiple personalities and dissociative diagnoses sometimes are placed in this category.

The DSM-IV (*The Diagnostic and Statistical Manual of Mental Disorders,* Fourth Edition) describes the BPD as having a pervasive pattern of instability of interpersonal relationships, self-image, and affects along with marked impulsivity, beginning by early adulthood. The BPD generally exhibits five or more of the following behaviors or characteristics:

- A frantic effort to avoid real or imagined abandonment.
- A pattern of unstable and intense interpersonal relationships characterized by alternating between extremes of idealizing and devaluing the other person.

- An identity disturbance evident by a markedly and persistently unstable self-image or sense of self.
- Impulsivity in at least two areas that are potentially self-damaging (e.g., spending, sex, substance abuse, reckless driving, binge eating). Note: this does not include self-mutilation.
- Recurrent suicidal behavior, gestures, or threats of self-mutilating behavior.
- Affective instability due to a marked reactivity of mood (e.g., intense episodic dysphoria, irritability, or anxiety usually lasting a few hours and only rarely more than a few days).
- Chronic feelings of emptiness.
- Inappropriate and intense anger or difficulty controlling anger (e.g., frequent displays of temper, constant anger, or recurrent physical fights).
- Transient, stress-related paranoid ideas or severe dissociative symptoms.

Borderline personality disorder appears four times more often in women than in men. This personality is frequently compared to the seductive and extremely dramatic histrionic personality disorder (HPD). However, where the HPD displays a superficial and theatrical behavior to maintain your attention, the BPD conveys a more intense passion to capture your soul. The histrionic may call you a devil, but the BPD believes you *are* the devil.

Remember ——————————————————————————

The BPD's paranoia is real. The BPD maintains control of others through passion, impulsiveness, intimidation, rage, threats of violence, and a profound neediness. Some people fall prey to this out of their own beliefs that they might help this poor wretch or as a result of their own weaknesses. BPDs see abandonment everywhere, intensely idealize or defame quickly, and become moody and enraged quickly, with paranoia always lurking just below the surface.

They do not know who they are and perpetually make poor decisions in terms of values, careers, relationships, sexual behaviors, and friends.

Remember

As with all personality disorders, first and foremost be aware of how the BPD makes you feel. Use this awareness and knowledge to deal with her rather than being used and manipulated. People with personality disorders use your feelings to control you. BPDs use guilt, intimidation, threats, and extremes of behavior.

The Contrasts That Confuse You
How People with Borderline Personality Disorder . . .

See Themselves	Want to Be Perceived
Intense	Loyal
Adoring	Wonderful
Whatever you want me to be	Justified
Entitled	Committed
Docile	Attractive
Needing nurturance	Passionate
Lost	Empty
Superior	Independent
Needing trust	Betrayed by life
Abandoned by others	Worthy
Fragile	Seductive
Mysterious	Desirable
Intriguing	Fascinating

How BPDs Will Appear to You if They Trap You

Intense	Experiencing unrequited love
Adoring	Always rejected
Compliant	Docile
Passionate	Confused
Needy	Appealing
Loyal	Misunderstood
Romantic	Harshly judged
Dreamy	Accommodating
Absorbing	Imaginative
Waiflike	Witty
Seductive	Devoted
Willing	Abused

How BPDs Will Appear to You if They Trap You *(cont'd)*

Used by others
Worthy
Easy
Flexible

Empty
Abandoned
Blameless

How BPDs Should Appear to You if You Are *Not* Trapped by Them

Intense
Volatile
Having no insight
Paranoid
Erratic
Impulsive
Quarrelsome
Unpredictable
Odd
Weird in how she sees things
Manipulative
Raging
Black or white
Ultracritical
Intolerant
Dependent
Sadistic

Demanding
Needy
Distrustful
Ultra-idealizing
Engulfing
Hypersensitive
Extreme
Turns people against others
Plays at always rejected
Moody
Does not get it
Indignant
Self-righteous
Overwhelming
Causing chaos
Controlling

Remember —————————————————————————————

How are they making you feel?

A TYPICAL CONVERSATION WITH A BPD: VILE VALERIE AND HAPLESS HARRY

After arriving from work and unloading groceries from his car, Harry washes up and begins to prepare dinner. Valerie has been depressed and in bed all day, a common enough event that Harry is not surprised that he will be making the meal. Valerie comes into the kitchen and sits down. There are Band-Aids on one arm.

Valerie: "I felt very alone today. When you're not here, I feel so empty. Why do you have to work such long hours?"

Harry: "Someone has to make money to pay the bills. Can't you call anybody when you're feeling down?"

Valerie: "No, I can't! I wish I could, but no one seems to want to talk to me. Why would I want to talk to anyone anyway? All they do is talk about themselves and don't care how I feel. Why did it take you so long to come home?"

Harry: "I stopped for some groceries. That was it."

Valerie: "No, you didn't. You stopped somewhere else. You're a half-hour later than usual. Maybe got a quickie with the checkout girl?"

Harry: "Huh?"

Valerie: "How often do you think of how better off you'd be if I were dead? My first husband tried to choke me to death once. Have you thought about it? I know you'd like to. What are you doing there? I should have killed myself earlier today instead of just cutting myself."

Harry: "Where do you get all this stuff?"

Valerie: "When I cut myself, it takes away the pain. You'll never understand that. I adore you. You are my life, but do you give me the love I need? No. You stay out and leave me here alone. I should be dead, that's how I feel anyway."

Typical Angry Response to the BPD

Harry: "You've spent the whole day in bed doing nothing. I'm trying to cook a meal, and you're ranting about your miserable life. You have no friends because you're such a bitch to them. It's not how they treat you; it's how you treat them. Your way of solving problems is cutting yourself and then looking for sympathy. Well, you can shove that. My friends who knew you before we got together warned me you were a slicer and dicer with your body, but I didn't believe it. You've sucked me dry. No wonder no one wants to be with you. Cut deeper next time."

Typical Guilty Response to the BPD

Harry: "Since I know how easily you're hurt and how angry it makes you, I try to do my best to please you. I know how badly people have treated you in the past, and I can understand why you feel the way you do from that. It must be so hard to trust others. You know I love you. My love will get us through this. Have patience with me."

How You Will Feel in Dealing with BPDs

At first . . .

Needed	"This person is so alone and empty."
Attracted	"She's so passionate."
Sympathetic	"So many people have hurt her."

Later . . .

Used	"This woman is very high maintenance."
Guilty	"I can't abandon her now."
Intimidated	"Maybe if I give in, she won't get so angry."
Confused	"Who is this person?"
Angry	"She has sucked me dry, burned me out."
Split	"When I look closely, she's got the whole family siding against each other and not her."
Afraid	"Will she hurt me in some way? Will she hurt herself in some way?"

How to Deal with BPDs:
What You Cannot Do

- Expect she will change.
- Be a savior ("My strength will make it work").
- Reassure.
- Argue and expect your point to be heard.
- Think you have made peace.
- Think you have an agreement.
- Get angry.
- Pout.
- Use guilt.
- Get physical.
- Be responsible for her happiness.

- Be responsible for getting her therapy.
- Get into power struggles.
- Romanticize ("Love will make it work").
- Romanticize your suffering.
- Keep behaviors a secret.
- Give more than you can.
- Make any big investments together.
- Lie for her.
- Get jobs for her.
- Feel guilty.
- Try to be the ideal she makes you to be.
- Believe you have worked something out.

Remember _____

For a BPD, you are either for her (love her) or against (hate her) her. There is no in between or compromising. There is no agreement about things in your relationship. You have no power.

How to Deal with BPDs
What You Can Do
(Do these mainly to keep your perspective.)

- Be direct in what you say.
- Explain your intentions simply.
- Repeat yourself a lot.
- Avoid arguments (the hardest); make a point and stay there.
- Keep it simple.
- Empathize.
- Stress that you cannot make her happy.
- Stay with what is real (do not argue with paranoia).
- Give structure if possible.
- Be direct.
- Be yourself.
- See relationship as it is.
- Call police (if abused).
- Call security (if at work).
- Inform everyone (friends, family, coworkers) what is going on.
- See your limitations.

- Be frustrated.
- Focus on the relationship as a continuum, not just on how it is today.
- Keep separate checking and savings accounts, credit cards, belongings (if unmarried).
- Expect the unexpected.
- Talk with a professional.

Remember

In dealing with a BPD, you must be very concrete and basic in what you say. And even then, it will be misunderstood and turned against you. A BPD is not your friend and definitely not someone with whom you can be intimate.

TYPICAL CONVERSATION: REVISED (AFTER HARRY READ THIS CHAPTER)

After arriving from work and unloading groceries from his car, Harry washes up and begins to prepare dinner. Valerie has been depressed and in bed all day, a common enough event that Harry is not surprised that he will be making the meal. Valerie comes into the kitchen and sits down. There are Band-Aids on one arm.

Valerie: "I felt very alone today. When you're not here, I feel so empty. Why do you have to work such long hours?"

Harry: "It has nothing to do with you. If I don't work, I don't get paid. It's as simple as that. You've been depressed for a while. That can't be fun."

Valerie: "I wish I had someone to talk to! No one seems to want to talk to me. Why would I want to talk to anyone anyway? All they do is talk about themselves and don't care how I feel. Why did it take you so long to come home?"

Harry: "I don't believe people are that self-absorbed. I know you do let your moods get to you and you can sometimes take them out on others. Relationships are a give-and-take. I stopped for some groceries. That was it."

Valerie: "No, you didn't. You stopped somewhere else. You're a half-hour later than usual. Maybe you got a quickie with the checkout girl?"

Harry: "That isn't me, and you should know that."

Valerie: "You're probably going to put some poison in the food to get rid of me. My first husband tried to choke me to death once. What are you doing there? I should have killed myself earlier today instead of just cutting myself."

Harry: "I know how bad you feel at times, but hurting yourself doesn't seem to me to be a way of feeling better. There must be other things you could do to cope better."

Valerie: "It takes away the pain. You'll never understand that. I adore you. You are my life, but do you give me the love I need? No. You stay out and leave me here alone. I should be dead, that's how I feel anyway."

Harry: "I like when you're happy and like to do things that make you happy, but you know I'm not perfect and I'm not the one ultimately responsible for your life. You are. We've had this discussion many times. I have no plots against you, and you should know that. You know I won't argue with your paranoia."

Valerie: "You think it's so easy to live life. People have ruined it for me. They keep turning on me."

Harry: "Living a happy life takes effort. I have to work at it every day."

THE TYPES OF PEOPLE WHO ARE MOST TRAPPED IN RELATIONSHIPS WITH BPDs

Relationships with BPDs can be so trying and difficult that it is difficult to imagine why someone (even a professional) would stay in this type of relationship. BPDs can exert tremendous charm, sexual appeal, and a seductive aura. This image usually is fleeting, with the BPD fiend emerging. Early on, we can be so confused as to how this incredible enchantress can so rapidly change that we stay on in the relationship, unbelieving that the raging person we deal with is really real.

Despite being raging, irritable, moody, and demanding, BPDs convey a profound sense of emptiness and need that they can use to appeal and trap others. They also use their rage or threats (of suicide, for example) to bind a person to them. Guilty and giving persons are trapped effortlessly by the BPD.

Families have to exert superhuman strength to avoid caring too much or being sucked into the guilty role. The BPD makes the family, especially Mom and Dad, out to be the ultimate reason for her suffering. The BPD sees her family as hateful, unkind, rejecting, and abandoning, when in truth it is only family members who might be willing to tolerate her.

BPDs readily ensnare the insecure male who is guiltified, manipulated, and bound to her. As with HPDs, the rescuers, especially professionals, believe that they will aid the BPD in her wretchedness and blame themselves when she is not made happier by their help. The much superior (in terms of manipulation) BPDs invariably chew rescuers up and spit them out, with the rescuers drained and angry from the experience.

Remember

You are to be her savior, her redeemer . . . but you will always let the BPD down, no matter how hard you try.

Remember

If it doesn't work, don't keep doing it!

SUMMARY

BPDs can be initially quite enticing and convey an intense and passionate connection to life. Alas, this connection is all black. BPDs are extreme, excessive, and unstable. They control with threats, rage, volatility, and a profound neediness.

CHAPTER 6

Pompous Egotist: The Narcissistic Personality Disorder (NPD)

Grandiose and Existing to Be Adored

"Thank you, everyone. I really do *deserve all of the praise."*

We have all come across people who think they are hot stuff. Narcissistic personality disordered individuals (NPDs) are the haughty, egotistical, and self-important people who see themselves as entitled and superior to the rest of us mortal creatures. Every day, we see in the media NPDs seeking (and getting) attention for their exploits, their fabulous looks or achievements, their money, their brilliance, or perhaps all of the above. Not infrequently in our daily lives, we also encounter NPDs who make attempts to convey their superior qualities to us. They usually put us off. But the better ones have the ability to manipulate and use us as they make us miserable in having to deal with them. Although it has now become a caricature of NPDs, a person saying, "Enough about me, what do you think about me?" truly identifies this personality disorder. In the NPD's mind, all conversations (as well as all of the world) should revolve around him.

NPDs include people of true achievement who need to have their egos constantly stroked. It is likely that their profound need for attention and adoration drove them to seek success in the first place. NPDs include also those without much going for them. These NPDs believe in their own brilliance without anything to substantiate it.

In either case, the NPDs are exclusively absorbed with themselves. What distinguishes NPDs from other successful or not-so-successful people is their pronounced need for admiration along with their sense of privilege to be treated in a royal way by everyone. An NPD truly believes that he or she is better than everyone else in every way. NPDs are absolutely self-absorbed and absolutely believe you should be absorbed with them too. They see everyone around them as reflections of their own glorious worth (like the king surveying his subjects to remind him of his power, or the father needing his son to be successful to reflect how brilliant a father he is). NPDs try to associate with only the "best people," since these others mirror their greatness. The NPD says, "I've gained a lot more respect for the pope after my private audience with him," while he is really thinking, "The pope and I make a great pair."

NPDs will associate with those of us they consider as inferiors so that we lowly humans can appreciate and be awed by their importance. The NPD thinks, *Look how great I am compared with these wretches that need ME, respect ME, envy ME, and idolize ME so much.*

Despite seeming like people from whom you would run, NPDs who are successful in life can trap you with their bravado, accomplishments, and success. As they describe their exploits, achievements, and triumphs, you are ensnared by feeling honored by the attention from this superhuman in your midst. The not-so-successful NPDs may also have a great flair for impressing you either by lying about their pasts or lying about imagined future plans and projects that make them appear to be movers and shakers. If you are not awed by the NPD, you will definitely be put off by the it's-all-about-me attitude. Either type of emotional reaction can make you prone to manipulation.

Remember

Whatever NPDs promise for you, it is all about them.

Red-Flag Feelings in You

Awe or intense admiration
Inadequacy and need for direction

Feeling special

Resentment or repulsion

Remember ————————————————————————

NPDs may be truly successful or not. They play into your sense of inadequacy.

Picture This

Who Are the NPDs You Might See?

You might spot an NPD if you notice the following types of behavior:

The woman who believes she should never have to wait. She's the first to say something like, "Do you know who I am?" . . . and really expect it to make a difference.

The person who cannot stop talking about himself, who is arrogant and rude to you and those around you. He has no clue about others' feelings unless you disagree with him. Then you get a rise out of him. He is verbally abusive when you might challenge his "right" to be the center of attention.

The person who lets you know she has done some great things. She has, for example, received honorary degrees or traveled extensively, has wealth or has written books, has received acclaim or done great works to help humanity. She has a charming way or fabulous looks. She has been successful in business or the arts. This person easily makes the rest of us feel pretty ordinary and inadequate.

A person who deliberately draws you in, since you are very likely to be awed by him (or react with envy).

The guy who exaggerates what he does to make it sound monumental. He might have been changing a tire, ordering pizza, or solving a simple problem at work, but he makes it sound like he was doing something extraordinary.

A person who might become surly and bad-mannered with you should you disagree or try to change the subject that interests her.

The speaker at your volunteer group who takes a lot of time to describe his background, schooling, and many achievements, even though it is not relevant to the talk. His lecture is amusing and charming. He sincerely conveys his profound interest in your needy cause and is quickly viewed as the savior for your group. He is not really interested in helping you, but rather looking for how he can look good by helping you. The woman who asks all about you only to relate these things back to herself. The guy at the restaurant who makes a scene if he does not get the right table or if his mashed potatoes are too lumpy. Special people deserve better.

Remember

NPDs are boastful, bragging, pompous persons who thrive on manipulating you, not just for your attention, but also for your adoration. Lying is not difficult for NPDs.

Picture This

Professional Life

NPDs do not seek you out professionally because they have a problem. Having a difficulty, a defect, or an imperfection for which they must seek help is unthinkable to them. Needing help is both demeaning and unacceptable to NPDs. They are too perfect.

Whatever the issue is for which the NPD is seeing you professionally, he will reframe it in a way that enhances his own prestige. First of all, he will identify you as an outstanding expert in your field, which allows the NPD to reassure himself that he mixes only with the best. He will then identify the situation in a way that can only lead to his self-aggrandizement. For example, if you are a physician and he has high blood pressure, he will consult with you because so many people direly need him to remain in excellent health and he is giving you the opportunity to participate. If you are a lawyer, he will meet with you not because of his legal problems, but because he is being thwarted by others from attaining his vision in some deal, or he is plagued by an undeserving and insensitive spouse who lacks appreciation of his greatness and largesse. If you are a counselor, he is seeing you to help someone else like his wife, a friend, or a family member. The NPD may seek help for anxiety or depression, but only insofar as it impedes his sense of controlling others. The NPD will claim to be "out of sorts." Never will his anxiety relate to his behavior or how he treats people.

NPDs exploit your role as an expert by appealing to your ego. An NPD will flatter you by elaborating on how she, worthy of the best of the best, chose you. She may embellish this by saying how so many other of her successful and knowledgeable friends also recommended you.

Remember

NPDs flatter you and elevate your status only *to advance their own and to control you. They have a total lack of sincerity, so be wary that their smooth talk does not go your head.*

Among the typical behaviors of an NPD are:
- Rapidly leading the conversation to his many accomplishments.
- Appealing to your vanity.
- Telling you how lesser professionals have let her down.
- Conveying somehow that he is giving you the opportunity to meet with him (this is a test for you to see how much you can add to his splendor).

Remember

The narcissist will follow what you recommend only if it feeds his ego in some way and/or allows him to manipulate others better. If you render any type of service, you are there to serve him according to his agenda that he will explain to you. Otherwise, you do not belong in the superior category.

This person will demand an appointment only when convenient. His belief is that everyone should stop what they are doing and turn their attention to him. No matter how actually important he is, the more you give in to his demands, the more likely that you will be exploited by him and be less professional than you would otherwise be. You can be so impressed with the NPD that you will bend the rules. After all, he is so successful, he knows better than you.

The NPD will adhere to what you recommend only if it does not require much effort. NPDs approach to treatment is: "You are the expert; make it go away, and do not involve me." All NPDs presume that they will be treated in a special way. Even in your professional role, because of the NPD's condescension and self-importance, you'll really have no authority in the situation.

Although the NPD may initially loudly idealize you, he will be the first to criticize you for letting him down, no matter how impossible the task or how little he cooperated with you.

True Life

True-Life Adventure 1:
Thomas Terrific, entrepreneur and man of the world, and Dr. Bob

A radio talk show had featured Dr. Bob, a psychiatrist, discussing stress management. Thomas, never called "Tom," called Dr. Bob for an appointment soon after the radio show aired to learn how to cope better with the stress of his busy life. "Not that I have trouble with stress personally. I'm a player. You should know that I'm worth over a million dollars. I function in a highly competitive and stress-filled environment. I believe that if I can master some new techniques, I'll be even better able to control the stress that others put on me," Thomas tells Dr. Bob in the first appointment.

"When I heard you on the radio, I was impressed with your knowledge and expertise," Thomas says. Without any prompting, Thomas continues, "I guess you need to know a bit about me." He tells Dr. Bob that he is a self-made high-roller businessman who books trade shows using soap-opera stars as attractions, that he is worth $2 million, what Mercedes he is about to buy, what gorgeous woman he had recently slept with (Thomas is still married), and how he manipulates his buyers by letting them be with the soap-opera stars. "These guys pay big money to stand and have their picture taken with some soap-opera bimbo," he tells Dr. Bob with a wink, indicating that Dr. Bob must understand how great men function.

Dr. Bob, conventional, mild-mannered, and soft-spoken, has trouble preventing himself from being awed by Thomas's success with money, business, and women. Thomas is living Dr. Bob's fantasies.

When Thomas, in describing his being victimized by others, volunteers some stressors in his life—like his going through his third divorce, his being investigated by the IRS, and his paranoia about trusting women—Dr. Bob nods his head in sympathy.

Thomas tells Dr. Bob, "All women are whores. They just try to use you. [Thomas's mother was a prostitute who brought clients home.] I give them everything they want without getting any of the appreciation I'm entitled to. You can't trust them."

Dr. Bob becomes taken with Thomas's man-of-the-world qualities. At one point, Thomas asks Dr. Bob to intercede for him in a relationship with a woman, and then Thomas would give Dr. Bob a "big Lincoln." Dr. Bob is trapped. He promises Thomas the very best treatment in relieving him of the stressors that "unfairly" vex his life. But in later appointments, Thomas admits that he was not faithful to his therapy and begins to instruct Dr. Bob on how things really should be run. It appears that Thomas cannot master certain relaxation techniques that require him to let go and relax because he always needs to be in control. Since Thomas cannot master the technique, which assails his grandness and perfection, Thomas leaves it behind. Dr. Bob has let him down. Thomas does, however, offer Dr. Bob a job as manager of Stress Management Treatment Centers, which Thomas is thinking of starting up.

Remember

NPDs resist change since it implies they have a problem. They will work with you as long as it enhances their self-glorification. They expect you to solve the problem, not them.

True Life

True-Life Adventure 2:
Naïve Nancy and Counselor Karen

Nancy, a young, bright, attractive lawyer in her early thirties, sought counseling with Karen. Nancy had a history of becoming involved in bad relationships in which she felt used and abused. Nancy wanted to find out why she did this so that she could have more gratifying relationships in the future.

"I know I'm intelligent, but I feel so dumb getting into relationships with guys who sweep me off my feet and who then get demanding and unreasonable," Nancy tells Karen. Nancy is presently involved with Neal, a handsome, personable, and very successful attorney for whom she works. Although things seem to be going well, Nancy's instincts are telling her that she might be repeating her past pattern again with Neal.

"He's incredibly brilliant when it comes to the law," Nancy says to Karen. "Neal is so successful. He tells me about the high-powered people he has as clients, the deals he puts together, and the influence he commands. I first met him when he taught in one of my law school classes. He tutored me and then, after graduation, he gave me a job so I could learn more from him. The relationship developed from there. Now he wants to get married," Nancy tells Karen.

Karen is wowed by Neal's importance and success. However, as Nancy further describes Neal and how he treats her, Karen wonders if Neal is more taken with himself than with Nancy. It seems to Karen that Nancy's role in Neal's life is to be his audience, not a potential partner. She shares her concerns with Nancy, who becomes more wary.

Nancy begins to see herself as falling into relationships based on her own lack of confidence. It seems that she needs to align with someone whom she sees as powerful and confident and on whom she can depend. When she becomes dependent, she then becomes controlled, used, and abused, since guys who look for dependent women excel at that. Nancy is now in a muddle: she wants to keep her job, but she also wants to extricate herself from this controlling relationship with Neal.

When Nancy tells him about her discussions with her therapist, Neal phones Karen. Karen tells him she can certainly listen to his concerns but cannot discuss anything confidential.

Neal tells Karen that he was the one who referred Nancy to her (unknown to Karen) because she came highly recommended as an outstanding therapist. Neal then describes his stellar background, his business successes, and his taking Nancy under his wing. "Nancy has blossomed professionally under my guidance," he says. "She can only grow more both professionally and personally with me directing her. I know she's had some bad relationships in the past. That's why I'm so good for her. I understand what she needs. I cannot understand why you don't see that."

As Neal continues lecturing to Karen, she notes to herself that he makes no mention of his love or concern for Nancy, nor does he ask what he might do to help. In reality, Neal has no sense of Nancy's needs, only his own: to be revered and adored. Karen knows that it is futile to tell Neal that Nancy has to learn to make decisions for herself and not have a tutor. Nancy needs to be a grown-up.

With bravado, Neal totally surprises Karen when he says, "If you'll put in a good word for me with Nancy and tell her to marry me, I'll buy you a new car." Karen thanks him for his offer and declines.

Remember

NPDs have a profound sense of entitlement. They have no empathy for others, and they presume that professionals should comply with their expectations—no matter how unreasonable they may be.

True Life

True-Life Adventure 3:
Righteous Robert and His Attorney, Dave

Robert, now in his late sixties, makes an appointment with Dave, his longtime lawyer, to make some changes in his will. Robert had been a very successful businessman who wheeled and dealed most of his life and was now semiretired. Dave has known Robert for many years and tolerated the man's haughty and demanding style only because it reminded Dave of what kind of person he did not want to be. Robert has been married and divorced three times and has children from each marriage. He had successfully driven his wives and children away by being overbearing, demanding, self-centered, and demeaning to all. Even some of the kids who tried working in the business left because of Robert's arrogance and inability to see anyone else's ideas but his own.

As they make small talk, Robert talks about feeling out of sorts, and he blames it on being semiretired. Dave sees that the problem is really the fact that Robert, at this point in his life, has no one around him who loves him. Because of his arrogance and pride, Robert is fast becoming a lonely old man surrounded by the best that money can buy but no one who cares.

"Why do you want to make changes in your will?" Dave asks.

"I never see any of my family. They don't care, so why should I? I want to drop them all from inheriting anything," Robert replies.

"Isn't that a little drastic?" Dave asks.

"I don't think so, and that's all that matters. They're all weak. They wouldn't accept my guidance or my advice. To hell with them!" Robert barks.

As they talk, Dave tries to broach the possibility that Robert's controlling behavior may have had something to do with his estrangement from everyone, but Robert will have none of it.

Finally, Robert narrows his eyes at Dave and pompously says, "You've been my lawyer for a long time. You know I've achieved my success and power from doing things my way. If you won't make these changes, I'll find someone who will, and that's that."

Remember

NPDs have a difficult time growing older. They find it harder to keep the audience coming back for more. If they are successful, they can use their money to keep people around and give them purchased attention. However, NPDs usually become more bitter as increasing physical debilitation intrudes on their grandiosity and they become less the center of the universe.

True Life

True-Life Adventure 4:
Bigheaded Bill and Peter, His Accountant

Peter, new to town and wanting to drum up some new clients for his just-opened accounting business, joined the local country club. He met Bill there when they played golf together. Throughout the game, Bill bragged about his executive job at a local corporation, the many activities that he participated in—like skydiving, scuba, and flying his own plane—and the many investments that had given him immense profits. Bill professed to know a lot of people in the area since he had volunteered for many organizations, which had presented him with humanitarian awards for his help. In between his rages about his poor equipment when he would hit a bad shot or miss a putt, Bill droned on about himself, leading Peter to believe that Bill was very accomplished and quite admirable in some ways, although extremely self-centered. At the end of their time together, Bill offered to spread Peter's name around as an excellent accountant and wondered aloud if he might call Peter for a consultation.

Some weeks later, the two men met together in Peter's office, with Bill bringing in several folders of papers about which he was seeking Peter's expertise. After reviewing everything, Peter was very impressed with what an idiot Bill was. Bill worked as an assistant plant manager in a factory and lived in a very modest home (Bill's only investment). Both Bill and his wife needed to work to feed their outrageous lifestyle, which was about to send them into bankruptcy. Bill did not volunteer his services, but had part-time jobs around town to earn extra money. He became incensed when Peter told him that he could not fix things up.

"There simply is not enough money coming in to handle your expenses," Peter told him. Somehow, it became Peter's fault that Bill led such a pretentious lifestyle beyond his means.

Bill became foul, demeaning, and insulting to Peter for letting him down. He left Peter's office with threats of spreading vicious rumors around town.

Remember

Whether successful or not, NPDs live in a world of fantasy. They are fragile and in need of constant praise and admiration. NPDs require your services as a professional to give praise and affirm their brilliance. You may give suggestions, direction, or advice, but it will likely not be followed. The NPD allows no criticism. Any assault to the NPD's self-delusion of perfection will evoke anger.

Picture This

Business Life

NPDs can thrive in the business setting. It is a win-win situation as long as the NPD performs, brings in the results, and gets his praise and stroking in return. However, if you have to work with NPDs, their aura quickly fades and you are left with the miserable situation of having to deal with their day-to-day pomposity. The business community will see the NPD one way if he produces; you will see him in another.

This person believes that he is the master and you are the slave. Businesses will see him as a leader.

This person exploits other people, but businesses see her as the supreme delegator.

This guy has no practical concept of the job but still may be viewed as "future-thinking."

This arrogant boob may be seen as self-assured and aggressive.

If she is only willing to associate with other high-status people or institutions, she may be seen as "bringing in the business."

This guy has no real concern for others, but the business world will view him as being a strictly bottom-line guy.

Your perception is that all the NPD wants is for people to agree with her, but in the business environment, she will be seen as always seeking others' opinions.

NPDs have a strong sense of privilege. As employees or coworkers, NPDs believe that they are gifted beyond everyone else. They will fish for compliments and expect special treatment in the form of contracts, projects, and favors right down to their desk, office, color of paper clips, and special parking spot. NPDs assume that their priories come first because they are bringing so much to the company; they believe that others, whether coworkers or higher-ups, should defer to them. NPDs will get irritated when others fail to assist them immediately in their "very important work." NPDs will overwork you and exploit you without any sensitivity of how it impacts on your life . . . and the hard work is not for the company; it is only to enhance the NPD's status.

An NPD believes that others are working because of their dedication to her. She, in turn, is not dedicated to you (either boss or coworker), her staff (if she has one), or the organization.

In situations where the organization is itself narcissistic and thrives on exploitation and manipulation, the NPD will flourish. In this setting, the company uses the narcissist to use others. Companies run by an NPD will exude selfishness and self-absorption from the boss who will surround herself with the best (but not better than she) and exploit others to enhance her magnificence.

Remember

NPDs are puffed-up and egotistical, lack genuine people skills, put others off, and cannot take criticism. The price of working for an NPD is your giving constant adoration and praise.

True Life

True-Life Adventure 1:
Marvelous Mike and Harold, His Boss

Mike joined a venture capital company a few months earlier as a vice president after wowing Harold, the boss, with his masterful style and list of accomplishments. Mike was quick to play up his own ideas as unique and brilliant while others thought his work was mediocre. Harold began receiving complaints about Mike's behavior. Mike was apparently making suggestions to senior managers in areas outside his responsibility, was openly critical of some people, and proposed elaborate, grandiose plans that were sure to fail. Mike was also poaching coworkers' clients socially.

When Mike's staff, who already felt exploited when he would take credit for their ideas, gave him feedback about some of his proposals, he became furious. He would attack anyone who did not agree with him and usually fire them. Mike was quickly destroying the cohesiveness of his department, and the morale was waning. The other vice presidents found Mike puffed up and condescending. Harold, confused over how this had occurred, sat down with Mike to discuss the complaints and his concerns about Mike's behavior.

Mike received Harold's comments poorly. He told Harold that many at the company envied him and were trying to make him look bad. If Harold understood this, he would then understand how untrue any criticism had been. Harold dismissed this notion. Harold saw that Mike had no insight into how he behaved, and Mike took no responsibility for causing the poor morale.

Curiously, after Mike left, morale and cohesiveness returned.

Remember

NPDs can be very destructive to a company. They lose sight of the organization's goals and are interested only in themselves. Because they are so self-centered, they cannot align with anything (or anyone) outside of themselves.

True Life

True-Life Adventure 2:
Dr. Star and Dr. Lesserman

Dr. Star had been the medical director of a large clinic for a few years. He then left abruptly "to follow other pursuits," although it was thought that Dr. Star was asked to resign under some shady circumstances. After that, Dr. Star adopted a position of strongly criticizing the clinic whenever he could for failing to meet the medical needs of the community, even saying that the clinic practiced bad medicine.

Dr. Star met with the new medical director of the clinic, Dr. Lesserman. During that meeting, Dr. Star told Dr. Lesserman about how busy he was professionally and about his new trophy wife and child, and he even invited Dr. Lesserman "to go sailing sometime—since we have so much in common as colleagues." Dr. Star then offered to consult to help the clinic to do a better job.

It amused Dr. Lesserman to think, *Here this idiot badmouths the place and all its people and then expects to get a job so he can do it more.*

After hearing from reliable staff members that the benevolent Dr. Star's patients were appearing at the clinic having been poorly treated, Dr. Lesserman again arranged a meeting with the great man to express his concerns.

Before Dr. Lesserman could speak, Dr. Star said, "You not only have bad information but consider your sources: your staff. I really would suggest that you get the true facts as they relate to issues that are brought to the clinic. As a respected medical doctor in this community, I am embroiled in medical care in the region and only seek the best for people in need. You have a truly wonderful opportunity to improve medical care for the citizens of our beautiful state, and I would hope that as a physician you would somehow trust the issues that another physician such as myself brings to you. I have made my recommendations to you already to set standards, communicate with physicians, treat patients with respect, etc., and I have told you I would be pleased to help you with this. I guess it's only natural to want to shoot me down, although all I want to do is help. I am fully aware that my statements or suggestions are assumed to be critical and not helpful to many individuals at the clinic. I have found that less confident people are put off by my constructive criticism. I would hope that you as the medical director and physician embrace my opinions, clinical expertise, and experience, and encourage input such as mine. It will only make your clinic stronger, your job easier, and your tenure as medical director more productive."

"Whew," Dr. Lesserman said to Dr. Star. "You sure rant on. Do people really listen to this garbage?"

Dr. Lesserman was astounded at how easily Dr. Star called others liars, deflected the subject of his doing anything wrong medically, and promoted himself as a medical visionary.

Remember ――――――――――――――――――――――――――

NPDs have inordinate self-pride. You exist only to mirror the NPD's greatness. He is your role model. If you confront him, he will see you as flawed. NPDs are blameless.

True Life

True-Life Adventure 3:
Amazing Al and Phil

It is Phil's first day on the job, and he is about to have lunch with Al, his new boss, who had actively recruited Phil to work under him. Prior to arriving, Phil had a difficult time getting various specifics about the job from Al and had to rely on Al's secretary. As he settled in, Phil still had a variety of questions but found Al unavailable.

As he sits to eat with Al, Phil thinks, *Now we can meet one-on-one and discuss some issues.* After they sit down, Al asks nothing about Phil, his move and relocating, or Phil's family. Instead of welcoming Phil and finding out his needs, Al immediately starts talking about the difficult time he has been having lately with his own bosses. Al is being investigated for possible mismanagement of company funds and will be starting a paid leave in a few days.

Nice of you to tell me now, Phil thinks.

Al then spends the entire lunch telling Phil about the shortsighted idiots in the company who do not appreciate his business prowess and who envy him. "That's why they're after me," Al reported. "I'm too good. I'm a big frog in a little pond of idiots."

Phil is filled with a number of emotions, but mainly he is angry that Al has smooth-talked him into joining a company that he is now badmouthing. Phil has relocated his family to work with someone who will now not be available, and the guy waited until he arrived to tell him. As time passes, Phil comes to see that Al got him to come in hopes that Phil would fail and show to management how important it is to have Al around.

Remember ————————————————————————

NPDs are entirely self-serving. They have no empathy. You cannot trust them.

True-Life Adventure 4:
Superlative Sally

Sally was a senior manager who thought herself a concerned boss. However, others doubted the amount of concern Sally had for her people. In meetings, for example, when the presentation went well, Sally did give compliments, but she did it in a way that said, "You made an excellent presentation that shows how well I'm running things. You are a reflection of my good judgment in having you on my staff." If the talk was less than perfect (and when the underling might need support and guidance), Sally distanced herself. Every meeting found Sally fishing for some sort of positive comments about herself, and if they were not forthcoming she would compliment herself without prompting. She loved to talk about the social events she attended and the important people there, her tennis game, and her goals for the company. She allowed little discussion in her meetings if it meant any challenge to her ideas. If you were not just a rubber stamp for her ideas, you were definitely out of the loop.

Although she joked and called people her "children," her "followers," or her "apprentices," and deemed herself "the chief," "the great leader," or "the mentor," everyone saw Sally as really believing that she was the great superior being leading those who adored her.

Sally had been grooming one of her staff members for advancement. The fellow was a bright and eager man who was taken with Sally's grandiosity. When an accident tragically killed him, Sally appeared crestfallen and in despair for a few days.

"How could he have done this to me?" Sally said. "I was helping him along, and he had so much yet to learn from me."

Remember

While seeming to care, NPDs will assume the role of a sensitive individual only because it is the thing to do. Meanwhile, they tell themselves what wonderful and feeling persons they are.

Picture This

Personal Life

The relationship with an NPD can be exhausting as you try to fulfill the NPD's insatiable need for admiration and praise. It can be like dealing with a very spoiled child who has tantrums when not constantly the center of attention. The NPD will initially woo you into a relationship by either recounting his exploits and successes to entrance you or courting you with flattery designed to make you think what a fabulous guy he is. However, once he believes he has ensnared you, the NPD then assumes that his aura should keep you around. He believes that he merely has to show up. In his mind, your being so grateful to be in his presence should drive you to keep the relationship going. If a problem develops, the fault is yours, because his greatness has no flaws.

Usually, the NPD's personal life is full of short-term relationships. NPDs seek out those who are vulnerable with self-doubt or who are in the process of needing direction. NPDs trap you by playing the brilliant chief, the tutor, the wise advisor, or the successful leader. This approach works particularly well with students, young people, those validly looking for direction (like learning how to be successful), and those who are unhappy with their own achievements. NPDs also play on your desire to do better. They hold out the bait of success to lure you in to being their pawns. Two NPDs getting together to exploit each other is not uncommon, but this situation is also usually short-lived since two selfish people cannot exist together for long.

Your being successful may initially be a draw for the NPD, who will view his being with you as a reflection of his worth. However, he will become competitive with you and attempt to make you feel guilty for doing well (that is, doing better than he is doing). As long as the NPD can keep his show of impressing you going, he can hold on to the relationship. When you begin to question or demand more in what usually is a very superficial relationship, or when you become more successful than he is, the NPD will break off with you with a dramatic show of his vexation in not being appreciated and venerated for his worth.

Remember

You exist to serve the NPD, who believes that you will sacrifice your needs for his comfort and support and expect nothing in return other than being in his presence. The NPD absolutely, positively has to be the center of attention.

In personal relationships, an NPD will exhibit behaviors such as the following:

- Blowing you away (or trying to) with his behavior and exploits.
- Acting full of herself. Everything she says is meant to impress you.
- Hanging many pictures of himself (along with anything that looks like an award or honor) in conspicuous places.
- Asking about you only to find out how well you followed her advice, or as a starting point to talking about herself.
- Always fishing for a compliment.
- Embarrassing you in public with his demanding behavior (he should not have to wait in line, he should have the best table, his drink was not exactly as ordered).
- Always having to say something to better you.
- Acting as if she has no flaws.
- Truly believing you only want to hear about him.
- Working hard on his agenda for approval, but being otherwise lazy. An NPD expects you to do all the day-to-day duties in the relationship or around the house.
- Expecting special favors without doing anything in return.

Remember

Royalty does not do windows.

True Life

True-Life Adventure 1:
Shallow Hal and Gretchen, Newlyweds

Gretchen met Hal at a tradeshow. Gretchen was modeling, and Hal, a brilliant inventor, was drumming up business for his newly formed company. Gretchen was immediately smitten with Hal's intelligence and drive toward being a successful businessman. Gretchen's own cleverness and beauty attracted Hal, who quickly grasped that she would be an excellent social resource for him. After a short courtship, they married. Since he was just starting his business and was not flush with cash, Hal talked Gretchen into a honeymoon combining travel across the country while Hal stopped at sites where he could market himself. Gretchen saw this as a romantic adventure (a honeymoon and helping her man) and agreed. Things went well the first day, with Hal going off in the morning and returning from his business at noon to spend the rest of the day with his new bride.

Bleak reality set in for Gretchen on the second day out. As the time passed into late afternoon and evening, Gretchen became increasingly upset. *Some honeymoon,* she initially thought. *My being cooped up in a motel room all day while he's out there doing things without me.* As time passed, she became more concerned about Hal. At eight in the evening, Hal showed up, and his explanation froze Gretchen. After leaving his business stop in late morning, Hal—so self-absorbed about his fantasies of success, power, and money—had simply driven on to his next stop. He had forgotten about Gretchen, his new bride, until later in the day. After recovering from her shock over this happening, Gretchen told Hal how upset she was. Hal dismissed Gretchen's anger, her being upset, and her sense of abandonment. He had no clue about the significance of such an action on the second day of their honeymoon. In fact, Hal became angry with Gretchen for not understanding the pressures on him.

As Gretchen was trying to deal with how distressed she was over the incident, Hal said, "I am doing all of this for you, and I expect you to be a team player. Great people have great demands made on them, and you need to understand that. My success is your success."

As the honeymoon progressed, Gretchen came to see that she was certainly not the number-one priority in Hal's life . . . maybe not even number-two. Nonetheless, she stayed married to him. She was in counseling for many years, trying to deal with her anger and loneliness.

Remember

NPDs have no feelings for others beyond how those people reflect the NPD's own greatness. You are a prop in a show where they are the stars. If you choose to stay with the NPD, make sure he is successful because, although you will be miserable, you will at least live a physically comfortable life . . . albeit an empty one.

True Life

True-Life Adventure 2:
Nell and Professor Luminous

Nell was a very bright, down-to-earth, small-town Minnesota girl who came to an elite northeastern university looking for knowledge, self-growth, and sophistication. She was a business major and did very well academically. In her senior year, she elected to take a class with Professor Luminous. The professor's reputation was one of a demanding and brilliant teacher from whom Nell felt she could learn much. He had a commanding presence in the classroom as he articulated his many opinions, intimidated his students with his knowledge, and flirted with the coeds. Nell immediately came under his spell and was thoroughly smitten with this brilliant and gifted man. Professor Luminous, in turn, was not surprised at Nell's awe of his charm and intellect (it had happened so frequently). He was also attracted to Nell's smarts and beauty. *I believe I can make this unpolished country girl into a real gem,* he thought to himself. He also loved the idea of having an exceptionally intelligent and beautiful young woman following him around.

After graduation, Nell, still in wonder of the man, stayed on as the professor's teaching assistant. They dated. They married. Nell felt honored as she attended the university social functions with the other acclaimed academics present. She was perplexed, however, with the professor's remarks. On one hand, he rhapsodized about all of the important people with whom he associated while, at the same time, he was critical and demeaning of the same people. She knew that the professor loved to be in the spotlight (which was easy in his classroom of captive students), and she felt he deserved it because of his achievements. However, she also saw that when he could not be the center of attention at the university gatherings, he pouted, became angry, and accused his peers of all sorts of imagined behaviors (their affairs with faculty wives, their plagiarism, their stealing data or mishandling departmental funds). Nell slowly came to see that, despite his accomplishments, the professor had an extremely fragile ego that constantly demanded feeding. He had to view all others as his inferiors so he could feel superior and confident.

Bright girl that she was, Nell began to see that even though she was his wife, the professor needed to keep her in her role of the admiring student adoring the brilliant professor. Trouble entered paradise as Nell emotionally and professionally matured and became more confident in herself. Things especially worsened in the marriage when she began to experience her own academic success. Nell was changing from the insecure young girl who accepted all of the professor's decisions into a self-assured woman. As this occurred and she dared to question him, Nell found the professor a raging, dogmatic, rigid, and arrogant person.

He questioned everything she did and tried to control all aspects of their lives—finances, decisions about the house, who they socialized with, when they went out, and so on. Yet the professor was lazy at home, as he could not be bothered with the simple chores of daily life. He felt that he was too important to be troubled with taking out the garbage, for example. Their sex life, which Nell had previously seen as less than passionate, was nonexistent. *When we made love, it was as though he was always watching his lovemaking in a mirror rather than becoming involved with me,* she thought.

The professor blamed Nell for any strife and treated her as a naughty child or a rebellious student for not obeying his wishes. "Why do you vex me so?" he asked her. "You know I always know what's right. I'll make all of the decisions for us." After some counseling (which the professor would not attend since he already had the answers), Nell sought divorce. Although regretful, Nell did not feel guilty because she knew she was right in wanting an equal say in the marriage, which was something the professor could never live with . . . and she could not live without.

Remember ———————————————————————

You are either a follower who feeds the NPD's insatiable need to feel adored, or the NPD sees you as an unappreciative and jealous rival.

True Life

True-Life Adventure 3:
Ken and Barbie

Not infrequently, two NPDs will couple up in a relationship. They have no genuine feelings for each other—each only seeing the other as enhancing his or her own status. Ken sees Barbie as attracting others to her, which means more potential attention for him to cultivate. Barbie, in turn, sees Ken having his own following, who will now notice her. Each exploits the other for more attention.

A variation of this situation is the NPD coupling up with another person who will bring implicit adoration to him. The classic example of this relationship is the boss marrying his secretary. He has already tested her on the job for selflessness, devotion, and catering to his needs. Why not continue it into his personal life? Other examples include the doctor and the caring, dedicated nurse; the professor and the adoring student; and, sometimes, the professional and the appreciative customer (think lawyer marrying the adoring client or the doctor marrying his admiring patient).

Remember ———————————————————————

No matter what he promises or what you may think is coming, all relationships with NPDs are superficial, and they usually fail.

True Life

True-Life Adventure 4:
Dr. Max the Magnificent and Wanda

Sometimes an NPD can hold us captive in a relationship because we think we need him for a particular service. As an example, Wanda had been seeing Dr. Max, her dentist, for a few years. He was a good dentist, so Wanda kept overlooking Dr. Max's bedside manner. He was loud and abrasive. He was always running late and gave the excuse that many important people sought him out; he just had to attend to them first.

Wanda would think, *What am I? One of the lesser beings?*

He frequently scolded his staff in front of patients. He always lamented his fate of being surrounded by less-than-able people, which also included his professional colleagues. "It's hard to fly like an eagle when you're surrounded by turkeys," he would lament to anyone who was in earshot. Wanda would think, *What an apt image, the turkey strutting around with his plumage out. Who could that be?*

Wanda tolerated Dr. Max's antics until one day when she made a return appointment to question some work he had done. Rather than being understanding and wanting to make it right, Dr. Max became high and mighty. He accused Wanda of not following his instructions and not appreciating the fabulous job he had done. If something was wrong, it had to be her fault. Dr. Max took no responsibility for what happened. Wanda thanked him and changed dentists.

Remember ———————————————————————————

We all like praise and dislike criticism. What distinguishes the NPD is his total love of praise and absolute intolerance of criticism. The successful person accepts criticism as a way of improving things. You have no say with an NPD.

DISCUSSION

In Greek mythology, Narcissus was renowned for his good looks and his pride. One day, Narcissus discovered his image in a pool and fell in love with his reflection. Narcissus thought the image in the water was real, and it became his heart's desire. Being able to love no one but himself, Narcissus pined away with desire and died there by the pool.

NPDs can be attractive, engaging, sociable, impressive, and likeable. Talking about their successes (or seeming successes), they can have an alluring charm. They create a striking picture of themselves that can pull admiration and awe from you, especially if they operate in an area where you want to be. The successes of others can be a big draw if you want to be in on them.

NPDs love only themselves. Their primary goal is to manipulate you into giving them constant adoration, approval, and admiration. Their need for attention and affirmation is unquenchable. NPDs attempt to trap you by impressing you with their exploits of one form or another, true or untrue. Once you are ensnared, you become a member of the fan club.

The DSM-IV (*The Diagnostic and Statistical Manual of Mental Disorders,* Fourth Edition) describes NPDs as having a pervasive pattern of grandiosity (in fantasy or behavior), a need for admiration, and a lack of empathy, beginning in early adulthood. The NPD will generally exhibit five or more of the following characteristics or behaviors:

- Grandiose sense of self-importance (e.g., exaggerates achievements and talents, expects to be recognized as superior without commensurate achievements).
- Preoccupation with fantasies of unlimited success, power, brilliance, beauty, or ideal love.
- Belief that he or she is "special" and unique and can be understood only by, or should associate with, other special or high-status people (or institutions).
- Need for excessive admiration.
- Sense of entitlement—that is, unreasonable expectations of especially favorable treatment or automatic compliance with his or her expectations.
- Interpersonally exploitative—taking advantage of others to achieve his or her own ends.

• Lacking empathy, and is unwilling to recognize or identify with the feelings and needs of others.
• Envy of others or belief that others are envious of him or her.
• Arrogance.
• Haughty behaviors or attitudes.

NPD occurs frequently in high achievers but also in those who achieve little. Even if successful (and frequently a profound need for attention drives an NPD to success), the NPD further exaggerates his accomplishments and believes himself a master of the universe. Life is about him, in the NPD's view, and you should drop everything else to comply with his wishes.

NPDs have no insight into their own profound need for veneration. They also have absolutely no understanding of other human beings' emotions or needs. The NPD believes that he or she deserves all the attention, while everyone else is undeserving. You exist solely as part of the fan club. The NPD justifies being haughty, rude, or arrogant by considering such behavior necessary to educate others about the NPD's importance and the treatment to which he or she is entitled. An NPD routinely overestimates his abilities, and is boastful and pretentious. He will unthinkingly assume that others also see his profound importance and will be surprised when the praise he feels he deserves is not forthcoming. The successful NPD usually has a well-oiled script that he follows in which he humbly (or not so humbly) describes what he has accomplished and then allows the oohs and aahs to gush forward from the crowd.

The NPD is extremely sensitive to criticism or defeat. She can feel marked humiliation although she would never show it nor admit to it within herself. She may react with rage and defiance or withdraw into pretended humility and acceptance. NPDs and ASPDs may seem similar in being personable and charming, but they are dissimilar. The NPD manipulates you because she needs others around to constantly praise and stroke her. The ASPD looks for attention so he can exploit you in other ways (money, sex, or power).

As developing adolescents, we all fall into the narcissistic category for a short time. This is usually a stage of development and does not necessarily mean the person will go on to become an NPD; ultimately, more men than women fall into this behavioral style.

You will find NPDs wherever human beings can be the center of attention: common places are the media, performing arts, academia, medicine, the pulpit, politics, police work, business, and entrepreneurial pursuits. Finding an NPD in isolating work, like a computer programmer, bookkeeper, accountant, forest ranger, long-haul trucker, or anyone who tends to work by themselves, would be rare indeed.

Typical behaviors of NPD individuals are:

- Attracting much attention to themselves in one way or another.
- Getting you to respond with envy, awe, admiration, or respect.
- Exploiting your desire and fantasies to achieve, or your sense of inadequacy compared with him.
- Controlling you by promising you the secret of success or by playing on your guilt for challenging his greatness.

Remember ―――――――――――――――――――――

As when interacting with all people with personality disorders, first and foremost be aware of how the NPD makes you feel. Use this awareness and knowledge to deal with the NPD rather than being used and manipulated. People with personality disorders use your feelings to control you. NPDs use their charm, their aura, domination, intimidation, guilt, and playing to your ego while inflating their own.

The Contrasts That Confuse You
How People with Narcissistic Personality Disorder . . .

See Themselves	Want to Be Perceived
A leader, a role model, an idol	Important
A visionary	An intellectual
Awe-inspiring	Perfect
Amazing	Astounding
Superior	Extraordinary
Special	Entitled
Successful	In charge
Charming	Irresistible

How People with Narcissistic Personality Disorder . . . *(cont'd)*

See Themselves	Want to Be Perceived
Charismatic	Admirable
Worthy of attention	Caring
Brilliant	Thoughtful
Humble	Understated
Giving	Self-sacrificing
Matchless	Unrivaled
Hypnotic	Captivating
A man among men	Adored by all
Fearsome	Intimidating
Attractive	Striking
Charismatic	Compelling
Entrancing	Enthralling
A go-getter	Considerate
Aggressive	Convincing
Righteous	Highly esteemed

How NPDs Will Appear to You if They Trap You

Leader	Modest
Role model	Praiseworthy
Visionary	Having keys to success
Idol	Hypnotic
Expert	A man among men
Teacher	Attractive
Awe-inspiring	Self-sacrificing
Unique	Magnetic
Charming	Persuasive
Successful	Caring
Gifted	Worthy
Insightful	Confident
Superior	Important
Brilliant	Highly esteemed
A person of the people	Unselfish
Humbling	Distinctive

How NPDs Should Appear to You if You Are *Not* Trapped by Them

Grandiose	Boastful
Pompous	Sneering

How NPDs Should Appear to You if You Are *Not* Trapped by Them *(cont'd)*

Moody	Shallow
Complaining	Tyrannical
Egotistical	Manipulative
Self-absorbed	Cold
Lazy	Condescending
Selfish	Disdainful
Uncooperative	Lying
Haughty	Vengeful
Boring	Unfaithful
Long-winded	Insensitive
Dominating	High and mighty
Controlling	Critical
Jealous	Rude
Blustering	Demeaning
Arrogant	Sneering
Paranoid	Amoral
Self-aggrandizing	Supercilious
Haughty	Self-righteous
Attention-seeking	Indignant

Remember ——————————————————————

Listen to your feelings in dealing with an individual with any personality disorder.

Remember ——————————————————————

If it doesn't work, don't keep doing it.

A TYPICAL CONVERSATION WITH AN NPD: YOU AND THE NPD

You: "Did you pick up the clothes from the cleaners? I left a note to remind you."

NPD: "There was a lot to do at work today. I had several important things to decide and many calls to make. People were asking something from me every minute. That new guy was being a show-off, so I had to do some staff education with him as a friendly one-guy-to-another-type thing. I think I'm being taken for granted at work."

You: "I guess that's a 'No' for the clothes?"

NPD: "I told you I have more important things to do than stop off at some cleaners. Can't you do it? I've got more important things on my mind, and I won't have you dictate to me what to do. When I agreed to let us live together, I told you that I don't do windows. You should know by now that I'm a big-vision guy."

You: "I told you this morning that I wanted to go to that exercise class tonight. I was hoping you could go to the cleaners before they closed."

NPD: "I'm always feeling fine except when I'm vexed by your unreasonable demands. When we met, I thought you had potential, but now I'm not so sure. . . . You're not home when I expect you to be, you expect unreasonable things from me, and you don't listen."

Typical Angry Response to the NPD

You: "What are you talking about? What *important* things do you have to do at work? You've had the same mediocre job for months. How many guys have already been promoted over you? As far as the big-thinker fantasy you have, all you do is sit and imagine yourself in some big office with people falling all over you. You're jealous and complaining about everyone else's success, but you do nothing yourself in terms of work. You pull me down whenever I have something good happen to me, and you make me feel that I am somehow beholden to you.

"And, yes, you should pick up the clothes from the cleaners. You should help around the place and not leave it all to me. You're just a lazy, crabby pain. I've had it!"

Typical Guilty Response to the NPD

You: "I don't know what came over me. I never meant to make you go out of your way. I can pick the cleaning up another time. I know you always have so much on your mind. I'm sorry for adding to it. Don't get mad. I'll get the cleaning tomorrow."

How You Will Feel in Dealing with NPDs

Awed	"He is truly amazing."
Charmed	"She is so witty, bright, and intelligent."
Flattered	"He's giving me his attention."
Enthralled	"Such an interesting person."
Intimidated	"She's much smarter than I am." "She's much more successful than I'll ever be."
Impressed	"Look what he's done in his life."
Insecure	"I hope I don't disappoint her."
Honored	"I'm privileged to be sought out by him."
Reverential	"She deserves more than I can ever offer."
Deferential	"It's okay. You're more important than I am."
Inadequate	"He's done so much and I so little."
Self-effacing	"I think I just want to disappear."
Annoyed	"This one is full of herself."
Indignant	"Who is this guy?"
Angry	"Ms. Superior, I presume?"
Puzzled	"Where is this guy coming from?"
Perplexed	"She *sounds* good, but something's not right."
Undermined	"For him, no one else can do anything of worth."
Indignant	"What an arrogant jerk."
Manipulated	"Suckered again."
Bored	"It's all about her. Like a broken record."

How to Deal with NPDs
What You Cannot Do

- Be overly awed by her achievements.
- Be flattered by his presence.
- Believe her praise of you.
- Work harder to win his praise.
- Expect intimacy.
- Feed her grandiosity.
- Believe his selflessness is real.
- Become financially or emotionally dependent.

How to Deal with NPDs *(cont'd)*
What You Cannot Do

- Expect understanding.
- Expect to gain something positive.
- Assume her responsibilities.
- Play into his entitlement.
- Accept her rudeness or condescension.
- Believe him.
- Lie to her.
- Set limits you will not keep.
- Overreact.
- Use sex.
- Try to control.
- Try to fix.
- Accommodate/adjust.
- Be endlessly giving.
- Cater to his ego.
- Think you will make her happy.
- Think *you* will be happy.
- See yourself as humble.
- Let him talk down to you.
- Give more attention.
- Feel inferior.
- Feel obligated.
- Be embarrassed by her.
- Accept him as better than you.
- Accept her using you.
- Compromise your values in favor of his.
- Feel ignored as a real person.
- Accept the blame.
- Expect her to take responsibility.

Remember

The NPD expects praise from you. Don't think that compliments are a way of handling an NPD. They thrive on them, expect them, and will be angry with you if you're not giving them the adoring praise they feel they deserve.

.How to Deal with the NPD
What You Can Do
(Do these mainly to keep your perspective.)

- Acknowledge everyone's (especially your own) right to the best.
- Acknowledge compliments (but don't let them go to your head).
- Be self-confident.
- Hold her to promises.
- Enjoy his show.
- Set limits (for yourself and her).
- Disagree.
- Contradict.
- Confront him with his arrogance (he will not change).
- Avoid some old arguments that you lose.
- Keep relationship superficial.
- Listen attentively.
- Use any leverage you have if she wants something.
- Be appropriately accommodating.
- Be firm in statements.
- Be practical.
- Be silent.
- Avoid being the mirror to his greatness.
- Seek others' advice.
- Follow your instincts.
- Leave.

Remember ————————————————————————

If you do the above, expect him or her to get worse.

Typical Conversation: Revised
(After Reading This Chapter)

You: "Did you pick up the clothes from the cleaners? I left a note to remind you."

NPD: "There was a lot to do at work today. I had several important things to decide and many calls to make. People were asking something from me every minute. That new guy was being a show-off, so I had to do some staff education with him as a friendly one-guy-to-another-type thing. I think I'm being taken for granted at work."

You: "I guess that's a 'No' for the clothes?"

NPD: "That's right. I was busy."

You: "There's no question that we all want to be irreplaceable at work, and I understand you need to do what you have to do. However, just like work, you have some responsibilities here that I believe are your fair contribution to our relationship. Helping out with errands, I think, is one of them. I get the impression that you think you're above doing the routine things of life, and that's unacceptable to me. We can discuss this anytime you'd like."

THE TYPES OF PEOPLE WHO ARE MOST TRAPPED IN RELATIONSHIPS WITH NPDS

NPDs can trap any of us into a relationship, because we all can become easily fascinated with someone who emanates (or seems to emanate) power, wealth, success, or charisma, which is what NPDs do. As they either carry on about themselves or have some lackey do it for them, NPDs can stir within us a desire to do better for ourselves, or they can evoke in us a feeling of inadequacy as we compare ourselves with these accomplished people.

NPDs know this and play on it. If you are willing to suffer the misery of dealing with an NPD because you will gain something (training, expertise, position, something more on your résumé), you may allow yourself to suffer as long as you do not lose your soul in the process and keep your perspective.

The insecure are particularly susceptible to an NPD's behavior because they are lured into a relationship thinking they need direction and guidance from this successful individual. The insecure person will be in awe of the NPD and willingly pay him the adoration he covets. If your confidence is low, the NPD will manipulate you into believing that you need him. All you have to do is idolize him. If you are unhappy with your own life and your achievement (or lack of it), the NPD will exploit that as he accents his own.

Giving people frequently are caught up in the NPD's web since they easily comply with someone who tends to take charge readily. Since NPDs offer themselves up as role models and as the ideal, abused people looking for a benevolent leader are also vulnerable. These individuals fantasize about the NPD taking them from a life of abuse but find themselves equally abused by a demanding and self-centered egotist.

Remember ————————————————————————

If you are into constantly stroking another's ego without getting anything in return—other than an NPD feeling that he is noble in letting you stroke him— the misery of NPDs is for you.

Remember ————————————————————————

If it doesn't work, don't keep doing it!

SUMMARY

Everyone wants success (the definition of which depends on who we are and what we hold as important), and NPDs use that desire in us to manipulate us into giving them homage and praise. If we already have some success or are looking to succeed, NPDs prey on us by promising more. If we feel less than adequate in our accomplishments, NPDs pledge fame and fortune.

NPDs are the consummate models of selfishness. They think only of themselves. The exception would be when considering that another person reflects well on them. They are grandiose and "special" and will constantly look to you to confirm this.

Conclusion

I hope you have learned some basic fundamentals about dealing with PDIs that you have carried away from this book. PDIs are everywhere in our daily lives, and it is inevitable that you will have some sort of interaction with them . . . hopefully a short one.

PDIs are masters of manipulation to their own selfish ends and use your feelings against you. They always provoke you in some way. When they get a reaction from you, they go to work to see how they can turn your feelings against you. If you have your own emotional baggage, PDIs use that to control you. If you are fairly well adjusted, PDIs exploit normal, healthy feelings. You cannot beat them at their own game because they do it so much better than you could, and besides, you would have to turn into a PDI to do it. Most often, you feel guilty and think that the cause of the problems lies with you. You get trapped into believing that if only you could do better, things will work out. *Say Goodbye to Your PDI* should have dispelled that mistake from your thought pattern and made you a much smarter observer of the users in this world.

In dealing with anyone you believe is a PDI, remember:

- Check your feelings. Being aware of how you are being provoked and that not being sucked in is your best protection.
- Avoid feeling guilty. PDIs love to hook you with guilt.
- PDIs never change, and you definitely cannot change them.
- PDIs are never wrong. They always blame others.
- PDIs are selfish and self-centered. It's all about them.
- There are actions you can and cannot take when dealing with PDIs.
- If it doesn't work, don't keep doing it.

Some people leave and some people stay in situations with PDIs. Because of your job, your profession, your family, or other circumstance, some of you will be obligated to deal with PDIs. *Say Goodbye to Your PDI* should show you how to cope better with them and give up the illusion that somehow you will change things for the better. Leaving the relationship, changing your job, or keeping a distance from certain family members are also options because, as you know, PDIs never change.

You can feel much more in charge of your life and with that sense of control comes a happier life.

Reference

The American Psychiatric Association. *Diagnostic and Statistical Manual of Mental Disorders,* Fourth Edition. American Psychiatric Publishing, 2003.

Index

About the Author

Stan Kapuchinski, M.D., is board certified in psychiatry and neurology. He was a dean's list undergraduate at New York's Fordham University. After being a National Institute of Health fellow at Cornell Graduate School of Medical Sciences, Dr. Kapuchinski attended St. Louis University where he received his M.D. degree.

He then pursued postgraduate training at the Boston University Medical Center in Internal Medicine and Psychiatry at the Institute of Living in Hartford, Connecticut.

Dr. Kapuchinski served in the U.S. Air Force where he held the rank of major and was department chairman of in-patient and out-patient psychiatry. While in the military, Dr. Kapuchinski also initiated a bio-behavioral program for psychosomatic illnesses.

While serving as a psychiatric consultant to numerous medical, business, and government organizations, Dr. Kapuchinski was a psychiatric volunteer in the Peruvian Amazon River Basin. Additionally, he functioned as Senior Psychiatric Specialist in Queensland, Australia.

Dr. Kapuchinski's health column, "Ask Dr. K," is presently published in the *Charlotte Sun Herald* along with a more tongue-in-cheek column, "Ask Dr. Bob, The Evil Twin," which addresses mental health issues in a more irreverent yet dignified manner.

Dr. Kapuchinski continues to practice psychiatry and write in southwest Florida as long as the law will allow. You can visit him at www.stopyour misery.com.

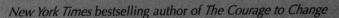